REALTIME
C OACHING

A Simple, Practical Approach for
People Who Rely on Others
to Create Results

RYAN LISK and RANDY LISK

RealTime Coaching
A Simple, Practical Approach for People Who Rely on Others to Create Results
Ryan Lisk and Randy Lisk © 2017

Print ISBN: 978-1-61206-133-7
eBook ISBN: 978-1-61206-134-4

Interior & Cover Design by: Fusion Creative Works, Fusioncw.com
Lead Editor: Roi-Ann Bettez

To purchase this book at highly discounted prices in quantities greater than 25 copies, go to Alohapublishing.com or email alohapublishing@gmail.com.

For more information about RealTime Coaching, visit LiskAssociates.com

Published by AlohaPublishing.com

First Printing
Printed in the United States of America

TABLE OF CONTENTS

NOTE FROM THE AUTHORS

In this book, we describe a particular method of coaching: RealTime Coaching™. It is applicable to an almost infinite number of situations. We are particularly indebted to the contributions of three people who have been instrumental in developing this system.

Dr. William Glasser, an American psychologist, developed Reality Therapy and Choice Theory in the 1960s. Reality Therapy helps people focus on their present and future actions as a way to create a better future for themselves. Glasser's work forms the theoretical underpinnings for RealTime Coaching.

In addition to Glasser's theoretical base, RealTime Coaching often uses personal assessments to better understand human motivation and behavior. We are indebted to Target Training International (TTI), based in Arizona and in particular, its founder Bill Bonnstetter. Bill was on the cutting edge of developing and providing the very best in valid assessments for over 30 years. He was a combination researcher, entrepreneur, and businessman who left a legacy of improving countless lives. His work lives on in TTI's products.

The third person, Ron Ernst, founder of Leadership Horizons, LLC in Carmel, Indiana, applied the work of these two giants in the industry to the coaching process. Ron focused in particular on applying Glasser's theories to organizations and businesses. Ron coined the term RealTime Coaching™. We began using Ron's work with our clients in 1994 and continue to use it today. In 1999, Ron published the first edition of his book *RealTime Coaching: How to make the minute by minute decisions that unleash the power in your people* (Leadership Horizons, 1999). RealTime Coaching has been of tremendous value to our clients. It is a simple, practical, usable, nonmanipulative approach to working with others.

In 2015, Lisk Associates purchased the RealTime Coaching intellectual property from Ron Ernst and Leadership Horizons. Our goal is to keep the material relevant to the times while being true to its basics. We hope you find RealTime Coaching to be as useful and durable as we have.

Ryan Lisk and Randy Lisk

SECTION 1

INTRODUCTION TO COACHING

INTRODUCTION TO COACHING

Since you are reading this book there is a good chance that you, like the many people we have worked with over the last twenty years, are somehow interested in getting things done, and helping others get things done. You may be an executive, a manager or a team leader. You may be a teacher or a nurse. You may be an attorney, a minister, a policeman, a mayor or a cattle farmer. Over the last twenty years we have worked with people in these professions and many more.

What is the common denominator we find among all our clients? They all succeed to the extent that they help others achieve their goals.

Some people we work with are just starting their careers and are looking for new tools to help them succeed. Others are more seasoned and are finding what used to work is not as effective as it used to be. We share ideas with our clients that help them work more effectively with others.

And now we invite you to explore this approach to coaching other people. It is built on simple ideas and based on sound theory. Over the past twenty years we have practiced these ideas in our business and have taught many others to use these ideas, with positive results on both a business and personal level. Welcome to RealTime Coaching™.

1 WHAT IS COACHING?

"It is literally true that you can succeed best and quickest by helping others to succeed."

—Napoleon Hill, author of *Think and Grow Rich*

According to various sources, the term "coaching" was borrowed from the name of the horse-drawn vehicle. The first of those conveyances was built in Kocs, Hungary, and was called a kocsi. When the kocsi came to England, the English translation became "coach."

In the 1830s, coaches were the fastest way for people to travel from point A to point B. Oxford students began using the term "coach" as a slang term for their tutors who helped them get through their exams quickly. The term became popular and is still in common use today. We like the image of the stagecoach, moving people along to where they want or need to go. That is the basic intention of a coach.

Coaching is the *process* a coach uses to help others achieve what they want to achieve.

Most people are familiar with the term coach as it applies to sports. During the last 25 years, more and more people have heard about non-sports coaches: people who deal with organizations or individuals. These people have job titles like life coaches, wellness coaches, executive coaches, management coaches, and more.

Coaching is an overt attempt to influence another person. There are various ways to influence others—some more effective than others. The RealTime Coaching method is consistent with our beliefs about ethically influencing people:

- When treated like reasonable adults, most people will respond in a reasonable manner.
- A person's behavior is their attempt to get what they want and to avoid what they don't want.
- Not all behavior is effective.
- People are responsible for their thoughts and behaviors, and can choose to change them.
- People respond better to support than judgment.

RealTime Coaching is a method for influencing and helping people based on these beliefs.

THE FIRST COACHING CONVERSATION

People succeed when they help others succeed. The human race has survived partly because we have banded together as a species for a very long time. Imagine this transcript from the first coaching conversation, held approximately one hundred thousand years ago:

> **Fred:** *I am so tired of veggies. I'd even eat that beast out there.*
>
> **Barney:** *Yeah, I'm with you. Enough with the greens. What are we, rabbits? But seriously, do you really want to take on that beast?*
>
> **Fred:** *I do. Problem is, have you seen the size of that thing? If I go after him I may end up being the entree.*
>
> **Barney:** *You could be right. Have you done anything so far to improve your odds?*
>
> **Fred:** *Well, I have been sharpening my spears and practicing my throws.*
>
> **Barney:** *That's good. Anything else?*
>
> **Fred:** *I've been pretty busy around the cave. There is always so much to do. But I have been thinking about going after that thing.*

Barney: *Well, if you just sharpen your spears and think about slaying the beast, will that be enough?*

Fred: *I guess not. What I really need is to be bigger. That animal is ginormous.*

Barney: *How likely is that? To be bigger, I mean.*

Fred: *Not very likely, I guess, especially on this diet of grass and weeds.*

Barney: *Is there anything you could do to appear bigger to that animal?*

Fred: *Hmm . . . Barney, you might be onto something. What if we both went after that beast? I would essentially be twice as big.*

Barney: *Now you're thinking outside the box.*

Fred: *What's a box?*

Barney: *Never mind. But I like your idea. Is there anything else you could do?*

Fred: *Well, I could invite some of the other guys to go with us. There will still be plenty of meat for everyone.*

Barney: *Can you get this organized?*

Fred: *Sure.*

Barney: *When will you do it?*

Fred: *I told you I was hungry. I'll get right on it and we'll go after that beast on the next new moon.*

Barney: *I can almost smell the barbecue.*

The first Lions Club Beast Roast was held shortly thereafter. Okay, we admit this is not an exact translation. Much has changed over the ensuing years, but the need for helping and supporting each other is still there, perhaps now more than ever. This book is a resource for those who want to succeed by helping others succeed.

Throughout the rest of this book, unless noted otherwise, when we use the term "coaching" we mean specifically RealTime Coaching and when we use the term "coach" we are referring to someone using that style of coaching.

2

THE COACHING MINDSET

"The key to effective leadership today is influence, not authority."

—Ken Blanchard, American author and management expert

Coaching is an attempt to *influence* another person. The people you attempt to influence will remember how you interacted with them. As you work with others, it is helpful to consider what kind of memories you are making. How will you be remembered by those you are attempting to influence?

There are various ways to influence other people—some more effective than others. To keep it simple, we call the three approaches to influencing people Do To, Do For, and Do With. To illustrate these approaches, let's say we have a roommate who does not keep our common area as neat as we would like. We would like to influence them to do a better job.

DO TO

Using a Do To approach we might say, "If you do not start keeping our common area clean, I cannot keep you as a roommate."

In other words, if you don't do what I want you to do, something bad is going to happen to you. This is one way to influence others. It uses fear as the motivator, and a real or perceived "up down" power relationship usually exists. The person making the threat is in the higher power position (parent, boss, police officer, landlord, doctor, drill sergeant) and the other person is in a dependent position. The person with the power is "doing to" the other person, who feels "done to" instead of respected and listened to.

In a Do To relationship, fear is high, trust is low. Although this approach can get short-term results, it damages any attempt to build a long-term, trusting relationship or to develop an adult-to-adult relationship.

No doubt, fear motivates people. And there are times when a Do To approach may be warranted.

"If you don't obey the safety rules, you will be fired."

"If you don't get your homework done, you will not graduate."

This approach should be used judiciously. Because Do To is fear-based, the problem comes when a Do To approach becomes someone's predominant style. Most people will not choose to live in fear over the long term. Most people, given a choice, opt for survival. In the case of Do To, survival involves getting away from the threat.

In a Do To department or organization, people who have the most options and alternatives—typically the "best" employees—usually leave first. This creates a downward spiral. As employees leave, the pressure to produce increases, increasing the amount of Do To influencing, increasing the level of fear, increasing the desire to leave, etc.

A Do To style does have legitimate uses as mentioned above, and it can create short-term results. However, if this style becomes predominant, these gains will be offset in time by losses from the resulting lower trust, higher turnover, and people "getting even." Our messy roommate may decide to clean up their room and stay, for now. Or, they may decide they can find a more accommodating, less demanding person to stay with somewhere else.

Peter Senge, author of *The Fifth Discipline*, said, *"There are only two fundamental motivations for change—aspiration and desperation."* Do To influencing uses and creates desperation. It can work in the short term. However, when people sense they are no longer in danger, they usually go back to their previous behavior. For example, most people who live through a heart attack do not change their lifestyle that may have contributed to the heart attack. For these reasons, RealTime Coaching does not employ a Do To approach to helping people make long-term changes. External control is not sustainable.

DO FOR

A second method for influencing others is Do For. Using a Do For approach, we might say to our messy roommate, *"I see you still haven't cleaned up our shared space, so I will do it for you."* Or, to put a business spin on it, *"Since you haven't completed your work, I will do it for you."*

You may be thinking, "Why would anybody in their right mind put up with that? Why would you let someone get away with not cleaning their room (or doing their job)? Who would do someone else's job?"

Or you may be thinking, "Hmmm, maybe I do that sometimes, but it is because I am so kind and want to help those other people. Also, if truth be told, I can do it better than they can. Plus, it is easier to do the work than to deal with the person who is supposed to do it. And I don't like conflict."

We tend to find the Do For approach to influencing (and managing) more prevalent with our clients than the Do To approach. Some professions such as nursing, teaching and nonprofits, to name a few, attract a Do For type of person who is motivated by helping others. People who belong to this category may not see themselves as Do For people. Do

For feels natural to people who live to help others. However, even for these natural givers, Do For can become tiresome and ineffective.

Think about the emotions people are feeling in a Do For relationship. What about the person doing the extra work? At first they may feel good about being a helper. Over time, it is more likely they will become frustrated. What about the person who is supposed to do the work? Most people want to feel as if they are contributing and earning their pay. They can feel micromanaged. They may think, *"What is wrong with the way I am doing it?"* They too can become frustrated, for different reasons.

When we discuss the Do For approach to influencing with managers, they often tell us the people at their company aren't like those "other employees." *"Our people just want to get by doing as little as possible,"* they say. We realize there are organizations that, over the years, have devolved into cultures of dependency. Also, we will concede that in most companies, three to five percent of the workforce have "quit but forgot to tell you" (*I Quit, But Forgot to Tell You* is the title of an excellent book by our colleague Terri Kabachnick).

However, we believe that for most people in most companies, this is not the case. Most people do not come to work thinking, *"Hmmm, how can I be mediocre today?"*

Peter Scholtes, a well-known consultant, was working with a company to help them improve. When he met with the top team, one executive said, *"I'll tell you what is wrong with this place. We've got deadwood."*

Peter responded, *"Why did you hire deadwood?"*

"We didn't hire deadwood," said the executive.

"Well, then what did you do to kill it?" inquired Peter.

The point is well taken: if you want to create dependent people, see them as dependent and treat them that way. The Do For style encourages people to *not* take initiative. Over time they say, *"Why try? My Do For manager will do it for me anyway."* We can practically see the deadwood stacking up. When this happens in a working relationship, the employee feels disregarded and the manager feels overworked. Neither person wins.

Do For can be, and is, a legitimate approach to influencing others. The following are examples:

- A new employee is learning a process. The trainer often demonstrates the steps or works alongside the new hire for a while.

- An employee has a personal emergency. Others in the department pick up the slack.

- A new person comes to live with us in our apartment. We show them how to keep things clean and picked up for the first week.

DO WITH

The third approach to influencing, Do With, is the answer to the question, *"What should I do if I don't want to use Do To or Do For?"*

Using a Do With approach, we might say to our messy room-mate, *"We are both responsible for this house. We agreed to keep it clean. Let's work together and get this place cleaned up."*

The Do With approach to influencing others is based on working together toward a common goal. A high-functioning sports team is a good example. Each member has separate responsibilities and assignments on the team. And yet, the team can't succeed unless everyone functions together. If one member misses an assignment, sometimes another member can cover for the error (Do For), but that is the exception, not the rule. There is a feeling of belonging, of contributing to something important. Trust among team members is high, as are expectations. It is not unusual in this environment for team members to hold each other to high standards of performance. Dependence is replaced by interdependence. A feeling of "have to" is replaced by a feeling of "want to."

A Do To or Do For environment discourages initiative. In a Do To environment, people think, *"I will only do what I am told to do, so nothing bad will happen."* In a Do For environment, people think, *"Why try? The boss (or parent, roommate, etc.) will do it for me anyway."*

Do To is a "hard" approach to influencing. Dr. Glasser referred to this style as "boss-managing." Do For is a "soft" approach to influencing. Neither is good for all involved. Both have their places. Both have their limitations. Do With is a "firm and fair" approach to influencing, what Glasser called "lead-managing." It is not necessarily quick or easy, but it is the clear winner in the long run.

It is never too late to start creating positive memories in the minds of those you influence. Coaching is an adult-to-adult relationship, based on mutual trust and respect. RealTime Coaching uses a Do With style of influencing others and can be summarized this way:

 COACHING MINDSET

It is my intention to use my coaching knowledge in a nonmanipulative way to work with others.

The people I coach are responsible for their own choices and behaviors. It is not my job to tell them what to do.

It is their job to choose what to do.

It is my job to assist them in making effective choices and following through on those choices.

3

REALTIME
COACHING MODEL

A Framework for Understanding
Human Behavior

"All models are wrong, but some are useful."

—George Box, author and statistician

RealTime Coaching (RTC) is founded on a theory of how and why humans behave as they do: their actions are an attempt to get what they want. We are indebted to Dr. William Glasser for his original work in this area.

RTC helps people get the *results* they want. Its underlying premise is *behaviors* create *results*. In other words, the effects of yesterday's behaviors are today's results. If you want to predict tomorrow's results, look at today's behaviors.

But what causes behaviors? Another RTC belief is that people are motivated to act (behave) in ways that either move them toward what they want (aspiration) or away from what they don't want (desperation). Personal *wants* cause *behaviors*.

If that is so, then where do wants come from? To answer that question, we acknowledge that each person is living in more than one "world." There is the world of external reality all people live in. This is the world we can all see, hear, touch, taste, and smell. It is the same world for everyone. But how each person perceives the external world depends on his or her own internal "world."

To understand this concept, all we need to do is observe two people reacting to a TV program. Both people watch the same show. The first person says, *"That was a great show."* The other person says, *"That show was horrible."* Both experienced the same external world. And yet, their internal worlds caused them to see it differently. As the saying goes, *You do not see the world as it is. You see the world as you are.*

Glasser used the term "quality world" to describe a person's internal world. He theorized that each person begins creating their own quality world soon after birth. As they grow, they accumulate a number of memory "pictures" that become the basis for how they want to satisfy their basic needs.

Glasser divided these pictures into one of three categories: (1) the people we want to be with; (2) the things we most want to own or experience; and (3) the ideas or systems of belief that govern our behavior. (For more information on this subject, refer to chapter three in the book, *Choice Theory: A*

New Psychology of Personal Freedom by William Glasser, MD (HarperCollins Publishers, 1999).)

It is as if there is a little movie playing in each person's head. No two people are showing the same movie. What is showing today is a result of all the experiences, of the nature and the nurture of the person, from birth to present. The movie seems real to the viewer—nonfiction.

The basic point is people's wants are created internally and separately for each of us in our own internal world. A person's internal world may be more familiar and, in many ways, more "real" to them than the external real world. Glasser believed people behave in an attempt to satisfy the wants of their internal world in the real external world. He said people were human *doings* more than human *beings*.

Notice the cause—*wants*—creates the effect—*behaviors*. Notice also that while a person's behaviors are visible in the external world (and to a coach), personal wants are invisible, existing only in the mind of the person—in their internal world.

Since wants are such an individual thing, an almost infinite number of wants exist in the world. But what causes the want? Various researchers have theorized that individual wants stem from a small number of *personal motivators* or basic needs.

Glasser listed four universal psychological needs, in addition to survival: belonging, freedom, fun and power. Another researcher, Eduard Spranger, in his book *Types of Men: The Psychology and Ethics of Personality* (Johnson Reprint Corporation, 1966) identified six "value attitudes," common to all people: theoretical, utilitarian, aesthetic, social, individualistic and traditional. A myriad of personal wants arise from a limited number of human needs. The RealTime Coaching model is based on this theory of psychology and an understanding of human wants, needs, and behaviors.

In summary, personal motivators create wants. Wants cause behaviors. Behaviors cause results.

PERSONAL MOTIVATORS ➡ WANTS ➡ BEHAVIORS ➡ RESULTS

Because of this cause and effect chain, people may or may not be eager to change their behavior, depending on the results they are getting. If a rational person is getting the results they want, it is likely they will continue their present behavior. If they are not getting the results they want, they can choose to (1) change what they want, (2) change what they are doing, or (3) evaluate the results they are getting differently.

With this basic understanding of human behavior, coaches can be helpful. What someone wants and how they judge the results they are getting are based on the internal forces and interests driving their personal motivation. Because others can't see these personal motivators and the wants they create, it is easy for others to misunderstand the resulting behaviors. A coach can help someone get the results they want by helping them understand the personal motivators behind their behavior and making adjustments as needed.

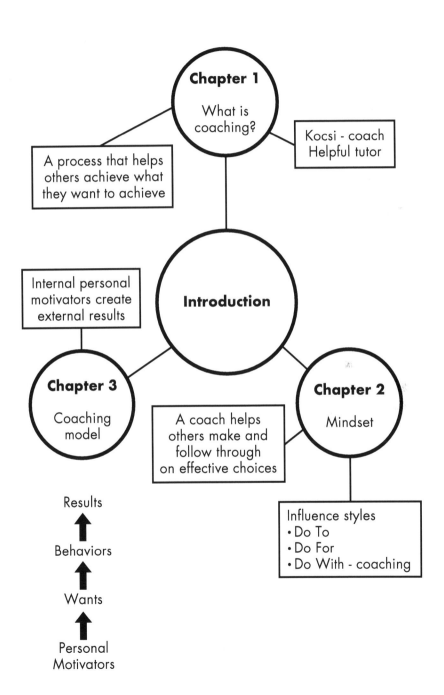

SECTION 2

FOUR BASIC COACHING QUESTIONS

Four Basic Coaching Questions

Putting the coaching model into action involves one or more conversations between a coach and a person being coached. In this book, we often refer to the person being coached as "coachee." We think this general term helps make the point that a coaching conversation can take place in almost any venue. It is not limited to a work environment. It may be between an employee and a manager, between a team leader and a team member, or between peers at work. Beyond work, coaching conversations are also applicable between a doctor and a patient, between two roommates (as we have illustrated), or between family members. The applications are almost endless.

Let us be clear that coaching is not therapy. It is not a substitute for clinical treatment. While coaching has a broad range of applications, we believe it is inappropriate and may be unethical to attempt to coach someone who needs a more clinical form of assistance. Coaches need to know where their boundaries are and need to be able to differentiate between the people who need coaching support from those who need something more.

Coaching conversations are of a specific kind. They incorporate four basic questions that focus on the four basic elements in the model. In the second part of this book we will explore those questions. Don't worry how to prepare for the conversation. We will cover that later. For now, just focus on the questions.

4

OVERVIEW OF FOUR BASIC QUESTIONS

"My greatest strength as a consultant is to be
ignorant and ask a few questions."

—Peter Drucker, American management consultant

Since the coaching conversation is the heart of the coaching
process, we will introduce the four basic coaching questions
now and then examine each one in greater depth. You can use
these questions in any order.

Just because we introduce a question first does not imply it
needs to be the first question asked.

1. WHAT DO YOU WANT?

Before a coach can help someone get the result they want, the
coach needs to know what result that person wants. A "want"

is a thought or desired outcome in someone's brain, so what someone wants is not usually obvious to an outside observer. Asking the "What do you want" question helps both people in the conversation frame the discussion. It encourages the coachee to hone in on what they *really* want and it makes evident to the coach the coachee's *real*, but often invisible "want."

2. WHAT ARE YOU DOING?

To quote Ron Ernst, *"You can't think or feel your way to a result. You must DO something."* A longer form of this question could be, **"What are you doing, or have you done so far, to get closer to achieving your goal?"** A coach encourages the coachee to *do* appropriate actions—to behave in ways that will help them achieve what they want.

3. IS WHAT YOU ARE DOING WORKING?

This coaching question allows—indeed demands—that the coachee evaluate their own situation and their progress. The longer form of this question could be, **"Is what you are doing getting you closer to achieving your goal?"** Notice that *the person being coached* does the evaluation. This *self*-evaluation is the cornerstone of the RealTime Coaching process. A coach is not a judge, critic, or evaluator.

4. WHAT IS YOUR PLAN?

This coaching question is usually asked toward the end of the coaching conversation. A plan of action, ideally created by the coachee, spells out what that person will do next to move closer to what they want to accomplish. A plan closes the loop, so to speak, to keep things moving forward. Without a specific plan, a coaching conversation can easily lack direction, lose momentum and become just another conversation.

HOW TO REMEMBER THE QUESTIONS

We use a simple mnemonic to help remember the four questions. We think of it as a radio station we can tune to. The call letters for the coaching radio station are WDIP. That reminds us of the four key words: Want, Doing, Is, and Plan.

> **The coaching "radio station" call letters are WDIP.**

Let's look at the cavemen's conversation at the beginning of the book and notice how Barney used the four questions when coaching his friend, Fred.

Fred: *I am so tired of veggies. I'd even eat that beast out there.*

Barney: *Yeah, I'm with you. Enough with the greens. What are we, rabbits? But seriously, do you really want to take on that beast? (W)*

Fred: *I do. Problem is, have you seen the size of that thing? If I go after him I may end up being the entree.*

Barney: *You could be right. Have you done anything so far to improve your odds? (D)*

Fred: *Well, I have been sharpening my spears and practicing my throws.*

Barney: *That's good. Anything else? (D)*

Fred: *I've been pretty busy around the cave. There is always so much to do. But I have been thinking about going after that thing.*

Barney: *Well, if you just sharpen your spears and think about slaying the beast, will that be enough? (I)*

Fred: *I guess not. What I really need is to be bigger. That animal is ginormous.*

Barney: *How likely is that? To be bigger, I mean. (I)*

Fred: *Not very likely, I guess, especially on this diet of grass and weeds.*

Barney: *Is there anything you could do to appear bigger to that animal? (P)*

Fred: *Hmm . . . Barney, you might be on to something. What if we both went after that beast? I would essentially be twice as big.*

Barney: *Now you're thinking out of the box.*

Fred: *What's a box?*

Barney: *Never mind. But I like your idea. Is there anything else you could do?* (P)

Fred: *Well, I could invite some of the other guys to go with us. There will still be plenty of meat for everyone.*

Barney: *Can you get this organized?* (P)

Fred: *Sure.*

Barney: *When will you do it?* (P)

Fred: *I told you I was hungry. I'll get right on it and we'll go after that beast on the next new moon.*

Barney: *I can almost smell the barbecue.*

Throughout the rest of this book we will provide many more modern-day examples of how to use the questions. Now let's take a closer look at each of the four questions.

5

COACHING AND PERSONAL MOTIVATION—WHAT DO YOU WANT?

"He who has a why to live can put up
with almost any how."

—Friedrich Nietzsche, German philosopher

THE DIFFERENCE BETWEEN FACTS AND ASSUMPTIONS

Let's take a deeper look at the "What do you want" question. As we mentioned earlier, everyone has their own personal inner world. What a person wants is their "why," based on their personal mental movie. However, if you were able to watch another person's movie, you would probably be confused. You might even have a role in this other person's movie, and you would hardly recognize yourself. Why people do what they do is not visible or obvious, even when we think it is.

We do people a disservice when we assume we know their motivations. *"I know why he is doing that"* is a phrase we often hear that, in most cases, is not true. A person making that particular statement has observed someone's behavior and jumped to a conclusion about that person's motivation based on their own personal inner world.

Instead of making that leap, competent coaches ask questions and listen closely to discern what is influencing someone's behaviors.

Although everyone lives in the same external world, they evaluate what is happening and decide what to do about it based on their internal world—their own movie. Sometimes, what shows up on the inner movie screen is mistaken for something in the external world.

To put it another way, there are facts and there are assumptions. A fact is something that exists in reality. Randy's granddaughter is eleven years old as we write this. That is true. It is a fact.

An assumption is anything *thought* to be true. It may or may not be a fact. It was created in the mind of the person making the assumption, but may not exist in reality. The statement, *"I know my granddaughter will do well in school this next year"* is an assumption. (Although Randy is pretty sure it will be a fact.)

As coaches listen to the people they coach, they try to discern facts from assumptions. Someone's strongly held assumption, positive or negative, will influence that person's behavior just as if it were a fact.

For instance, a person may say, *"I want to be project leader, but I know Frank is trying to prevent that."* A coach hears that statement and helps that coachee evaluate it. Is it a fact or an assumption? The coach might respond, *"What have you observed that leads you to believe Frank is out to get you? Could there be another explanation for his behavior?"* This kind of question helps the person self-evaluate and notice their assumption. When a person acts on an incorrect assumption, their behavior will not be in line with external reality. That is often the source of their problem.

As coaches listen to the stories people tell, they can ask themselves questions to help them recognize facts versus assumptions.

- How is this person interpreting their experience?
- Are they a participant or a bystander in this experience?
- How does this person assign meaning and importance to this situation and outcome?

What conclusions has this person drawn? Are the conclusions based on verifiable facts?

While exploring their wants, people may find that what they thought they wanted was based on an incorrect assumption.

After they question the assumption and decide it is not a fact, their want automatically changes, or the supposed roadblock disappears. For example:

Coachee: *I want to be project leader, but I know Frank is trying to prevent that.*

Coach: *What have you observed that leads you to believe Frank is out to get you?*

Coachee: *Every time I am talking he interrupts me with some crazy idea.*

Coach: *Every time?*

Coachee: *Well, not every time. But, you know, he acts like his idea is always more important. He makes it hard for me to stay on track.*

Coach: *Does Frank interrupt other people or just you?*

Coachee: *Hmmm. Thinking back I guess he interrupts people a lot of the time. Yes, other people too.*

Coach: *Is it possible when Frank interrupts you he is just being Frank—no pun intended?*

Coachee: *I guess it is possible. Maybe I overreacted. You think I should push to be team leader?*

Coach: *What do you want to do? There will still be Frank, or someone like him.*

And on it goes . . . .

"WHAT DO YOU WANT?" CAN BE A DIFFICULT QUESTION TO ANSWER

It seems like such a simple question. However, when we ask someone, "What do you want" the answer often comes back, *"I don't know"* or *"What do you want me to do, coach?"* Neither of those answers helps the person focus on what they want. Several issues may be preventing them from giving a clear answer.

1. There may be a low level of trust in the relationship between the coach and the coachee. Perhaps they just met. Or, the coach may be in a managerial position above the person being coached. In these cases, the coachee may not feel comfortable divulging their want. They may think, *"The coach may use my answer against me."*

2. The person being coached may not have thought clearly about what they want. They may not know what they want, but they probably know what they *don't* want. Coaches listen for the "don't want" answers and deal with them quickly.

Coach: *What do you want?*

Coachee: *I'll tell you what I don't want. I don't want to have to work with Frank.*

Coach: *Okay, I understand you and Frank are having issues, but I am still curious if there is something you **want** to happen.*

Steve Morris, a friend and colleague of ours, is fond of responding, "Do you go to the grocery store with a list of things you don't want to buy?"

3. Sometimes there are two or more conflicting wants in the mind of the coachee. This may be because there are competing personal motivators. A person might say, *"I like my job. I get to help others. And yet, I want to make more money than I can in this job."* Perhaps that person has a high personal motivation to help others along with a high personal motivation to get a fair return on the investment of their time. Coaches help people sort out these competing wants, once those wants have been identified.

4. People sometimes give up on their wants or dreams. *"I'm too old to go back to school,"* or *"I'd like to start a business, but I've only got ten more years until retirement,"* are not uncommon responses we hear. In essence, the person is thinking, *"People will think I'm crazy, so I just won't mention it—or act on it."*

We are not advocating that everyone go back to school or start a business. But we do believe that people who have a strong desire (want) to do something, no matter how crazy it seems, will probably be better off to talk it out and either decide to do it or forget it. The "dream," even if not mentioned by the coachee, may be keeping that person from a 100 percent commitment to any other want.

A coach who senses there is a "hidden want" that a person is hesitant to divulge may say, *"If you could wave a magic wand, what would you do (or create, or be, or what would you change)?"* The magic wand gives the coachee permission to "create" something out of the ordinary.

5. There are usually several layers of "wants" in the mind of the coachee. As a coaching conversation continues, what the coachee says they want will often change. In that case, just having the conversation is helping that person clarify their thoughts and wants. Coaches can help people discover deeper wants by: (1) listening for what is not said as well as what is said; (2) allowing the person being coached to explore their thoughts at their own pace.

Here's a simple example:

> **Coach:** *What do you want out of your job?*
>
> **Coachee:** *What I want is for my boss to get off my back.* (This is a "don't want" answer.)
>
> **Coach:** *Okay, you don't want your boss to hassle you. I don't blame you there, but is there something you **do** want from your job?*
>
> **Coachee:** *I just want a paycheck.*
>
> **Coach:** *That sounds reasonable. What does your paycheck allow you to do?* (looking deeper)

Coachee: *I'm a single mom with two kids and a mortgage. I need to take care of my family.*

Coach: *Your paycheck lets you take care of your family?*

Coachee: *Yes. At least the basics. Things are still tight sometimes.*

Coach: *So your job lets you take care of your family. Is there anything else you want from your job?*

Coachee: *I don't know. I haven't really thought about it.*

Coach: (pauses)

Coachee: (after some silence) *I like the inspection part of the job. I'd like to do more of that, particularly if I got paid to do it.* (smile)

And on it goes. Coaches listen closely for what may be hiding underneath the initial response to "What do you want" because that deeper "want," when identified, will help move the coachee forward.

VARIATIONS ON A THEME

Coaching is not an exact science like mathematics. In this book, we offer many suggestions and approaches for exploring the four basic questions with a coachee. They all work some of the time. Hardly any of them work all the time. That's what makes coaching so interesting. People have free will, and a wide variety of wants.

The Want question does not even need to contain the word "want." For instance:

- What would a perfect (fill in the blank—meeting, job, project, marriage, day, boss—) look like to you?
- If we get together here, six months from now, what would you like to be different or better?
- Can you describe the gap between the way things are now and the way you'd like them to be?

These are a few thought starters. We are sure you can come up with better examples. *What would a perfect Want question sound like to you?*

Another of our favorite coaching questions is in response to the answer, *"I don't know."*

For instance:

Coach: *What do you want to happen here?*

Coachee: *I don't know.*

Sneaky coach: *I know you don't know, but if you did know, what would it look like?*

That may sound like it would never work. Just try it. Say it calmly as if it were the most natural question in the world. You will hear a plausible answer about half the time, because many times coachees do know. But, for whatever reason, they are reluctant to say it. Of course, sometimes a person actually does not know the answer.

This kind of coaching response works for any of the four basic questions.

> **Coach:** *What is your next step? (a Plan question)*
>
> **Coachee:** *I don't know.*
>
> **Coach:** *I know you don't know but, if you did know, what would your next step look like?*
>
> **Coachee:** *I guess I'd go talk to Frank.*

Another way coaches can help the coachee discover what they want is to use the tried and true feedback approach of Start, Stop, and Continue.

> **Coach:** *I'd like you to think about your job (or your team, your department, whatever the issue is) over the past few months and identify the activities you have done that*
>
> - *You are not now doing but would like to **start** doing,*
> - *You get little or no enjoyment from and you would like to **stop** doing, or*
> - *You are doing now and you would like to **continue** doing or do more of.*

DEVELOPING AUTHENTIC QUESTIONS

We've shown some variations on the basic "What do you want?" question to show how it can be used. As coaches sharpen their skills, they develop their own list of coaching questions that are variations of the basic four. Obviously, it would be a rather strange conversation if a coach just used the same four questions over and over. Part of what makes a good coach is their ability to be authentic.

Everybody says things in different ways. A question one coach uses all the time could easily feel weird to another coach. No problem. Don't use that question. For instance, we mentioned the "magic wand" question earlier. It works for us, but it may feel awkward to others. The best questions arise out of the context of the conversation. However, when preparing for a coaching conversation, it never hurts to jot down two or three questions for each of the WDIP questions, to help the conversation begin smoothly. After that, the better the coach listens, the better the questions get.

BASIC HUMAN NEEDS INFLUENCE WANTS

When you are thirsty, you want a drink. When you are tired, you want to rest. These are physical wants that arise from basic bodily needs. Similarly, when some people have an opportunity to learn something new, they jump at it. Others don't. When some people get a chance to work extra hours for more pay, they jump at it. Others prefer to go skiing. Just as our bodies have physical needs, there are a few underlying psychological needs that influence what we want. Just as there are differences in physical needs from person to person, there are also differences in psychological needs. While the specific wants a person has change over time, the underlying need influencing that want stays relatively constant.

For instance, the person who likes to learn may have had deep interest in a special subject such as biology or mathematics in high school, did extra research for projects in college, got fascinated by what allows bumblebees to fly, and took their first job developing drones that deliver packages for Amazon. The underlying basic theoretical need to learn stayed constant throughout the person's life, influencing what the person wanted and, therefore, what they did.

We mentioned a couple of models of basic human needs earlier in the book. Glasser and Spranger, as well as other researchers, have posited similar but slightly different lists of basic needs. As researchers develop ways to monitor and interpret the workings of the brain, we are confident the answers to the question of why people do what they do will continue to evolve.

For our purposes, it is not so important for coaches to know a precise list of basic human needs. We will leave that to the researchers with their high need to learn. It is important for coaches to understand the connection between a person's basic needs and what they want, because without that understanding, the coach is left to guess—or worse yet—make assumptions about the coachee's motives.

In our coaching work and coaching workshops, we use a simple, reliable online assessment developed by our partners at TTI to help us and the coachee understand their basic needs. It is based on the work of Spranger. We have included an overview of this assessment in the Resources portion of the book.

> **A want is an attempt to fill
> a basic human need.**

WHY CAN'T WE ALL JUST GET ALONG?

Spranger theorized six different "value attitudes" that affect our basic needs. Considering all the possible combinations of these six value attitudes, chances are good that people will have different sets of basic needs and, thus, different wants. These differences show up in the external world as "differences of opinions."

Here's how these different needs might show up in the workplace. Imagine a group of executives discussing whether or not to provide a new benefit for the employees. The CFO, who has a passionate basic need to always get a good return on investment, thinks it is obvious and natural to not provide this benefit unless there is a sound business case with adequate payback. He says something like, *"It is just good business practice to require a business case to justify this new benefit. No margin, no mission."*

The VP of human resources, who is passionate about helping others, weighs in, *"People are more important than things. We will not survive if we don't have a positive people bottom line."*

The director of research, one of our theoretical friends who is always searching for more data, wonders aloud, *"Could we just stop and check online to see what others are doing?"*

The CEO, driven by a basic need to be in charge, wonders to himself, "I wonder why they don't just do what I say?"

Disagreements are a normal part of group work. Sometimes the disagreement happens because all parties don't have the same information.

> **Exec 1:** *I heard there was going to be a layoff. I can't believe the corporation is so heartless as to fire our people after the loyalty they have shown. And at this time of year.*
>
> **Exec 2:** *Hold on. We are not "firing" anyone. Data from HR indicates there are a number of employees who would jump at the chance to retire early with a very generous package. It will be totally voluntary. Financially the company can do it now and get prepared for the future. It is a win-win.*
>
> **Exec 1:** *Voluntary. Huh. I guess I heard it wrong. Sorry.*

Disagreements that arise because of lack of information, or misunderstood information, are relatively easy to solve. Values disagreements are more difficult to solve. The reason they are so difficult is internal-world differences show up in external-world conversations as not just *differences* but as personal *attacks*. One person thinks the bottom line is the most important thing. Another person will take a hit to the bottom line to provide a benefit to the employees. These two people are operating from two different basic needs–two different internal worlds.

Many of us recognize the phrase *"We hold these truths to be self-evident"* from the US Declaration of Independence. The problem is, everyone is equipped with their own set of truths. The good news is differences can not only create chaos, they can also create synergy. A diverse group will usually make better decisions, particularly on complex matters, as long as they work in an environment of trust and mutual respect. Coaches can be especially helpful during values disagreements by encouraging participants to be "hard on the problem and soft on the people."

WHEN NOT TO ASK THE "WANT" QUESTION

We end this section with the reminder that there are times when it is not necessary to ask the Want question. Someone may walk up and say something like, *"I need some help thinking through how to get the Smith Project wrapped up on time. Can you help me?"*

This may sound like a great time for a coaching conversation. The person asking for help has stated what they want. And, although that want may change during the conversation, it is probably not a good time to respond by saying, *"Okay, tell me what you want."* They will likely think, *"I just told you. Weren't you listening?"* Instead, you could ask for more background—what still needs to be done, or what part of the project is under the most pressure, etc. The next coaching question would likely be, *"So what have you done so far to keep the project on schedule?"*

That is a Doing question, so let's take a closer look at that question in the next section.

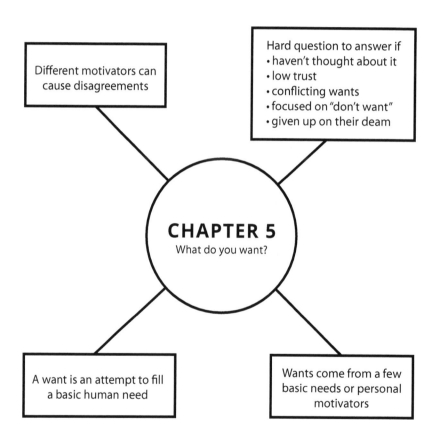

Different motivators can cause disagreements

Hard question to answer if
• haven't thought about it
• low trust
• conflicting wants
• focused on "don't want"
• given up on their deam

CHAPTER 5
What do you want?

A want is an attempt to fill a basic human need

Wants come from a few basic needs or personal motivators

6

COACHING AND INDIVIDUAL BEHAVIOR STYLES—WHAT ARE YOU DOING?

"The way to get started is to quit talking
and begin doing."

—Walt Disney

WHY ASK THE "DOING" QUESTION?

Coaching is about helping people change behaviors. The Doing question encourages people to focus on what they are doing—their behavior. As mentioned previously, everyone lives in both an internal and an external world. Their internal world provides a mental image of what they want. Behavior is what a person uses to close the gap between what they want and what they perceive they are getting. Many people see their internal world more clearly than their external world—

the "real" world. In that case, they are often more aware of their intent than of the effect of their behavior on others.

What a person wants is *why* they behave. Their behavioral style is *how* they behave. When we speak of behavior we are specifically talking about action—doing or not doing something. Behavior can be captured by a video recording.

> **Observable behavior is a person's attempt to close the gap between what they want and the results they perceive they are getting.**

The question, *"What are you doing to get what you want?"* helps people focus more clearly on their actions and the consequences of those actions.

For example, from our cavemen's earlier conversation we heard, *"Have you done anything so far to improve your odds?"* And the follow-up, *"That's good. Anything else?"*

DOING AND NOT DOING

When we ask people, *"What are you doing to get what you want?"* we often hear answers such as, *"I've been thinking about it"* or *"I need to finish something else first, and then I'm going to…."* In other words, they have actually done very little. The Doing question helps people make sure they are actually doing something, and not just thinking about doing. Coaches ask the Doing question, along with the Plan question, to encourage people to take useful action.

DOING REFERS TO BEHAVIOR COMPLETED IN THE PRESENT OR RECENT PAST

Doing is not about ancient history. Coaches are generally not interested in the past. Coaching is not some form of therapy where a lot of time is spent reliving a person's childhood. Yesterday's behavior is what got the person to where they are now. They can't go back and change that past action. The past may be useful to coaches as a way to help identify part of the coachee's internal world—how they see things—and if there are patterns of behavior that repeat themselves. However, coaches do not want to listen to history unless it is pertinent to what the person has done recently or is going to do next.

> **Coach:** *I understand the quality of the work you are doing is not quite up to standard. The framistats you assemble have a number of defects—more than those of your coworkers.*

> **Coachee:** *I guess, if that is what the records show. But I work fast and get a lot done. I have always been a fast worker. I had a third-grade teacher who told me I got my work done first. I was the fastest one in class.*

> **Coach:** *Interesting. So, what have you done to improve the quality of your work in the job you have now? It doesn't sound like being fastest without acceptable quality is what is needed.*

DOING IS NOT PLANNING FOR FUTURE ACTIONS

Just as the Doing question does not refer to the past, it also does not apply to the future. Future behavior—that not yet enacted—is planned behavior. As you may remember, another of the WDIP questions—the Plan question—focuses on future behavior. Coaches do not accept planning answers to Doing questions.

> **Coach:** *We've met a couple times to talk about the quality of your work. What have you done so far to improve it?*
>
> **Coachee:** *I think we're going to change suppliers on the main body of the unit. That should make assembly easier and improve quality.*
>
> **Coach:** *When will you have those parts?*
>
> **Coachee:** *I'm not sure. I just heard some guys talking about it.*
>
> **Coach:** *Sounds like that might make a better product in the future. It is not helping you now, right?*
>
> **Coachee:** *Right.*
>
> **Coach:** *I'm more interested in what you have done in the past couple of weeks to raise the quality of your work to an acceptable level.*

I DON'T HAVE TIME

When we ask, *"What have you done?"* we often hear the response, *"I haven't had time to . . . ."* People are busy. And yet, we

60

are asking about what the coachee has done to get closer to something *they* have said they want. Part of a coach's work is to not accept excuses while being respectful of the coachee.

In our coaching workshops, we sometimes do an exercise we learned from our friend Skip Murray. We ask people to fill in five blank spaces under a heading that says: **I Don't Have Time To. . . .** You might mentally do this right now. Think of five things you don't have time to do.

In the exercise, we then ask participants to draw a line through the words, **"Have Time"** and write in above them **"Want To."** Then the list becomes five things—usually these are personal tasks—under the heading, **"I Don't Want To."** It is a sobering exercise, and some cry *"not fair."*

Maybe it isn't fair. We then ask, *"If I gave you a thousand dollars if you did one of the things on your list, could you find time to do it?"* Usually the answer is *"Yes."* Then we ask if it is a matter of no time or a matter of priorities. Or maybe it is just easier to say, *"I don't have time"* rather than the more truthful, *"I don't want to."* Coaches should not accept excuses, including *"I don't have time"* without checking on and challenging that statement.

Another aspect to this response occurs when we are encouraging new coaches to learn to coach by doing it. We sometimes hear the *"I don't have time to coach"* answer. Of course, we discuss that with them as well.

CONNECTING INTENTION WITH IMPACT

Ralph Waldo Emerson said, *"What you do speaks so loudly I cannot hear what you say."* As we said before, people may not be aware of the impact of their actions. The Doing question helps shed light on that.

We often use this quote in our work: *"There are two experts in every conversation. I am the expert of my intention. You are the expert of my impact."* In other words, my intention is in my internal world: what I want or intend. My impact is how my behavior affects you and others. My intention is not visible to another person. My impact on the other person is not directly visible to me.

For instance, we intend to write this book to be a usable, practical manual for people wanting to learn more about coaching. People who read it will determine the impact of this book on them. The Doing question can help people better understand their impact on others.

Coach: *So what did you do next?*

Coachee: *I went to Frank's office.*

Coach: *What happened then?*

Coachee: *I told him I didn't appreciate him interrupting me in meetings all the time.*

Coach: *How did Frank respond to that?*

Coachee: *Not well. He got all defensive and said something about me hallucinating.*

Coach: *So, exactly what did you say to him? If I had been there what would I have seen and heard?*

Coachee: *What are you saying? It's my fault he got in a snit? That's nuts.*

Coach: *No. What I'm saying is it sounds like you did not get the response you expected or wanted from Frank. Perhaps part of the reason for that is the way you talked to him and what he heard. Is that possible?*

Coachee: *I suppose. I just don't think I should have to sugar-coat my words to Frank.*

Coach: *You don't have to do anything. And yet, if you really want to improve your relationship with Frank, and it sounds like what you are doing is not working, it seems like you might want to examine your approach.*

Coachee: *Okay. I didn't intend to irritate Frank. We're both busy. I don't like to waste anybody's time with a lot of chitchat. I just got right to the point. I said, "Hey Frank, got a minute?" He said, "Yes." And then I said, "I don't appreciate you interrupting me in meetings."*

Coach: *We both know Frank is very conscientious about his work. He can take a neutral comment and hear it as a criticism. It sounds like you were direct with Frank. From our work together, I know the direct approach works for you. However, if you were to have that conversation with Frank again, can* *you think of a different way to open the discussion that might not put him on the defensive?*

And on it goes. . . .

VARIATIONS ON A THEME

As is true with each of the WDIP questions, it is important for coaches to have a few alternative Doing questions available to make the conversation go smoother. Some examples might include:

- "What are you doing to . . . ?"
- "What actions have you taken?"
- "What did you say to Frank?"
- "How much have you completed?"

With just a little practice, coaches develop their own list of Doing questions. And, as we said before, the context of the conversation will provide hints to the observant coach about what to say next.

USING ASSESSMENTS TO RECOGNIZE DIFFERENT BEHAVIORAL STYLES

People have different behavioral styles. Some are introverts, some are extroverts. Many are "ambiverts," displaying characteristics of both introverts and extroverts. Some people are more results-oriented while others are more people-oriented.

Some are patient, some are impatient. These and many other behavioral characteristics are manifest in the huge palette of different human behaviors. When coaching, it is useful to be able to identify different behavioral styles in order to better understand others' behavior and be able to communicate effectively with them. Assessments are a helpful way to identify behavioral styles.

There are a number of different behavioral style assessments on the market. We often use an assessment from our partners at TTI based on the well-known Dominance, Influence, Steadiness, Compliance (or DISC) model. It is valid, reliable, and easy to complete.

If you want to learn more about the DISC model, we have included an overview in the Resources section at the end of the book. In addition, the reliability, validity, and adverse impact studies for the assessments we use can be found on our website: LiskAssociates.com/selection.

With a model like DISC to follow and just a little bit of study, most people are able to identify their own behavioral style as well as that of others. With this knowledge, coaches can improve their communication and influence with a wider range of people. People being coached can get insights into their own behaviors as well as how to modify their preferred style to better communicate with others.

An assessment also makes it easier for a coach to notice when a person seems to be in a role, such as work, where the behavior required seems to be much different than their natural behavior. For example, a person may be an introvert but, for whatever reason, lands in an extroverted job (such as a salesperson). They literally become a different person, behaviorally, in that role. They are "wearing a work mask." Perhaps they can keep the facade up for a while, but it takes energy, and that behavioral mismatch may cause other problems. Also, we humans are not very good at hiding our true feelings. Other people can read them in micro-expressions on our face, even if it is on a subconscious level. This mismatch comes across as being not authentic. When people see the difference between how they naturally choose to behave versus how they behave in a key role such as at work, it is often eye opening.

WHAT'S NEXT?

We have examined two of the four coaching questions: (1) What do you want? and (2) What are you doing? It is easy to see how they work together. If a person *wants* something, they must *do* something to get it. The next question helps people check to see if what they are doing is helping them get closer to the results they want.

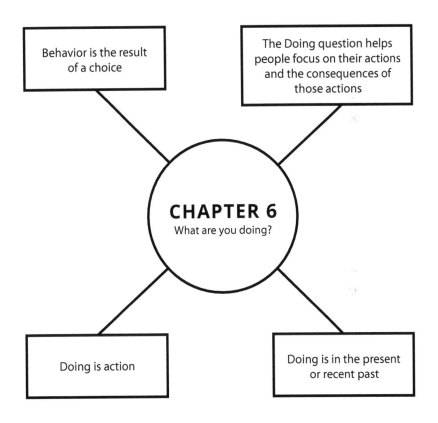

Behavior is the result of a choice

The Doing question helps people focus on their actions and the consequences of those actions

CHAPTER 6
What are you doing?

Doing is action

Doing is in the present or recent past

7

COACHING AND PERSONAL ACCOUNTABILITY —IS WHAT YOU ARE DOING WORKING?

"When you judge another, you do not define them, you define yourself."

—**Dr. Wayne W. Dyer, American self-help author**

WHY ASK THE "SELF-EVALUATION" QUESTION?

One dramatic difference between RealTime Coaching and other approaches is the use of self-evaluation. This is the Is question in the WDIP call letters. People being coached evaluate their own behavior and its results. Coaches do not evaluate. Coaches withhold judgment and help the people being coached examine their wants, perceptions and behavioral choices. Coachees state what they want and what they have done or are doing to get what they want. Then *they* evaluate their own situation and decide whether things are getting better or worse.

Of course, each person's perception is heavily influenced by their internal world. A coach may silently agree or disagree, but it is the job of the person being coached to evaluate their own progress. When people evaluate their own situation, they take a step toward reclaiming their independence and a step away from being a dependent victim. This may be surprising, or even difficult, for some people. Perhaps they have worked for some time for a Do To or a Do For boss.

For example, we once heard a manager say, *"We hire 'em from the neck down."* In a workplace culture which holds that belief, the company is paying for the whole person, but only using their hands and backs. The head and heart are being wasted, or likely engaged somewhere else. Imagine the culture shock the coachee might experience if a new Do With manager/coach were to come in. It would take patience and encouragement from the new manager/coach to help people reclaim their independence.

The self-evaluation question speeds a transition to independence. One sign of dependence and/or fear in the workplace is a reluctance of the coachee to speak up.

Coach: *Is what you are doing working?*

Coachee: *I don't know. What do you think?*

70

Coach: *I'm more interested in your own assessment. Do you think you're making progress?*

CHECKING THE MISMATCH BETWEEN WANTS AND PERCEPTION OF RESULTS

The coaching model we described earlier says wants create behaviors, and behaviors create results. One way to visualize this idea is to use the image of a balance scale. Balance scales are used to calculate the weight of an object. Two plates are connected by a balance beam (similar to a playground teeter-totter). The object to be weighed is placed on one plate of the scale and a known weight is placed on the other plate. The scales balance when the correct weight is placed opposite the object being weighed.

We borrowed this image for coaching. Imagine a balance scale with "what someone wants" on one plate and "what they think they are getting" (their perception of current results) on the other plate. When the scales are in balance, they are getting the results they want. If the scales are not in balance, there is a difference between what they want and what they think they are getting. They are not getting what they want.

Our coaching model says intrinsic motivation, the inner desire to do something different, occurs when people have "unbalanced scales"—when what people want is not what they perceive they are getting at that time. Therefore, people can "balance their scales" (get what they want) by changing their behavior.

A coach who wants to help someone change their behavior will first make sure the coachee's scales are *not* in balance. Or, as Ron Ernst says, *"Comfort the afflicted, and afflict the comfortable."*

> **The difference between what a person wants and the result they perceive they are getting is the motivation for all behavior.**

VARIOUS WAYS TO USE THE "IS" (SELF-EVALUATION) QUESTION

Coaches can use the self-evaluation question in a number of different ways. We have broken these alternatives into a few separate categories.

EVALUATING WANTS AND PERCEPTIONS OF REALITY

Asking the self-evaluation question can help the coachee check the mismatch between what they want and their perceptions of reality. For example, in our cavemen's conversation, when Fred said, *"What I really need is to be bigger,"* Barney, the coach, replied, *"How likely is that, to be bigger, I mean?"* Coaches can use other questions to help people evaluate their perceptions, such as this:

- Is what you are doing getting you what you want?
- Did your preparation pay off?

- Did you get what you wanted from Frank?
- You said you wanted to be a team leader. Will complaining about the amount of extra work you have help you get there?

EVALUATING DIRECTION AND PACE OF PROGRESS

The self-evaluation question can also help people realistically gauge their progress. Again, from the cavemen's conversation, Fred said he had been *"sharpening my spears and practicing my throws." Barney*, the coach, asked in reply, *"Well, if you just sharpen your spears and think about slaying the beast, will that be enough?"* Following are examples of other questions coaches can use to help coachees evaluate their progress.

EVALUATING THE USEFULNESS AND ATTAINABILITY OF THE GOAL OR WANT

We stated earlier that the four coaching questions can be asked in any order. When the coaching conversation is focused on what people want, the self-evaluation question can help them decide if what they want is possible to attain.

- Is your goal realistic?
- Is it helpful for you to look at it that way?
- How does your plan fit with what the rest of the department wants to do?
- What does a win look like in your mind?

EVALUATING THE IMPACT OF BEHAVIOR

We mentioned in the last chapter on Doing that a person is often more aware of what they want (their intent) than they are of what they are doing (their impact). Misunderstandings between people that do not get checked out or challenged are a prime reason interpersonal issues occur.

Coaches can help the people they coach "shine a light" on the impact of their behavior. Coaches do this by asking skillful self-evaluation questions, such as

- What do you think George thought about what you said to him?
- If I had been there, what would I have heard (or seen)?
- Is it possible Frank misunderstood your tweet?
- What did Allison's reaction tell you?

When people being coached recognize their impact on another person was not what they intended, they are far more likely to choose more effective behaviors.

SIMPLIFYING THE SELF-EVALUATION

Sometimes when we ask for self-evaluation—*"Are things getting better or worse?"*—the person being coached says, *"Yes and no."* In that case, we've learned the person is so intimately involved with whatever they are working on that it naturally seems complex to them. Some things are better, and yet there are these other things . . . .

Coaches can help clarify that kind of situation by injecting some objectivity and simplicity. When someone is having a hard time boiling it down to whether, overall, things are better or worse, we recommend saying something like, *"It sounds like you are dealing with a very complex situation. However, as you consider your overall present situation today, compared to two weeks ago, is it a plus, a minus, or a zero?"*

Obviously, a "plus" means things are better, a "minus" means things are worse, and a "zero" means things are the same. This answer may be all that is needed to make a plan for the next steps. Often self-assessment does not require a high level of precision to be useful.

We have discussed three of the four WDIP questions. Notice how the three questions—What do you want? What are you doing? and Is what you are doing working?—relate to the metaphor of a balance scale. The person being coached evaluates the balance. That person, not the coach, determines whether their behaviors are getting the results they want.

One piece of the process is missing. After people evaluate their current status, they need to decide what to do next. That brings us to the fourth question.

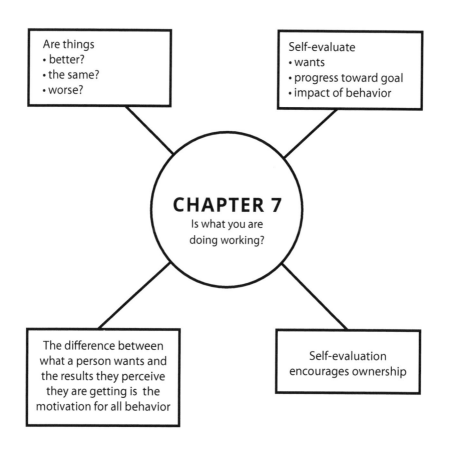

Are things
• better?
• the same?
• worse?

Self-evaluate
• wants
• progress toward goal
• impact of behavior

CHAPTER 7
Is what you are
doing working?

The difference between
what a person wants and
the results they perceive
they are getting is the
motivation for all behavior

Self-evaluation
encourages ownership

8

COACHING AND FOLLOW-THROUGH— WHAT IS YOUR PLAN?

"If you don't know where you're going,
any road will take you there."

—The Cheshire Cat in Lewis Carroll's
Alice in Wonderland

"If you don't know where you are going,
you'll wind up someplace else."

—Yogi Berra, American baseball player

WHY ASK THE "PLAN" QUESTION?

The Plan question closes the loop on the coaching process. In other words, the first three questions help people being coached evaluate both what they want and their recent behavior, so they can determine what behavior they want to use going forward. They can then decide what to do next to keep working toward their goal. The Plan question helps people be accountable for doing what they say they are going to do. The Plan question also keeps the coaching process moving forward rather than stalling out or going in circles.

As a manager a number of years ago (before he learned coaching), Randy had conversations with his employees to get them "back on track." These were good people. They would thank him for his guidance. About three weeks later he would often see the same ineffective behaviors from the same good people. Without an agreed-to plan, he found himself having essentially the same conversations over and over.

WHOSE PLAN IS IT?

Ideally, the coachees create their own plans. Coaches support, encourage, and help people focus on what to do next. It is not the coach's plan. When people evaluate their present situation (by asking themselves: Is what I am doing working?), they strengthen their independence. When people create their own plan, they further strengthen their independence. This is a great example of how coaching uses a Do With approach.

A person may be reluctant to come up with a plan and may even say they "don't know" what to do next. This may be true in a few instances. For example, the person may be new in the job.

In most cases, though, we have discovered that people may be reluctant to state what they know needs to be done next. It may be something they don't want to do. It may be something they think won't be well-received. Or, they may be used to their boss/coach telling them what to do, or doing it for them.

Here is how a coach might handle that situation.

Coach: *So, what is your next step?*

Coachee: *I'm not sure.*

Coach: *You said you want to have a better relationship with Frank. Is that still true?*

Coachee: *Yes.*

Coach: *Let me ask you, on a scale of one to ten, with one being not important and ten being very important, how important is it for you to have a better relationship with Frank?*

Coachee: *Hmmm, maybe a seven or eight. Things at work would be a lot better if we worked better together.*

Coach: *So that is pretty important—a seven or eight. Since it is so important to improve this relationship, what do you need to do next?*

Coachee: *I guess I need to talk to Frank again, in a better way for him. But I feel stupid. I don't really want to do it.*

Coach: *What are the odds of the relationship improving if you don't talk to him?*

Coachee: *Not very high, I guess.*

Coach: *Okay, so could you do it? Could you have the conversation, even if it might be difficult?*

Coachee: *I guess so.*

Coach: *Would you have this conversation with Frank?*

Coachee: (Pause) *Yes. I don't think the relationship will improve unless I do.*

Coach: *That sounds right, based on what you've told me. When will you have this conversation? How about sometime before we meet a week from now?*

Coachee: *Okay. I'll do it.*

Coach: *And we can discuss how it went when we meet next week?*

Coachee: *Yup.*

Coach: *We've got some time left. We could work on what you might say to Frank if you want.*

And on it goes . . . .

COULD YOU, WOULD YOU, WHEN WILL YOU?

In the conversation above, the coach first asked if the person *could* have the conversation with Frank. This allowed the person to begin considering the possibility of doing it. It is a low commitment. Next the coach asked the person, "*Would* you . . ." This increases the level of commitment. Finally the coach asks, "*When will you* . . ." to make the next action very clear. Using this could you, would you, when will you approach, the coach provides focus and support so the person can create a plan. These three questions are adapted from the well-known *Sedona Method: Your Key to Lasting Happiness, Success, Peace and Emotional Well-Being*, authored by Hale Dwoskin (Sedona Press, 2015).

A WORKABLE PLAN CONTAINS EFFECTIVE BEHAVIORS

Coaching is about helping people identify and implement more effective behaviors. These behaviors will help them achieve their goals. A useful plan contains at least one specific behavior that will move the coachee closer to their goal.

Competent coaches can answer the following questions at the end of a coaching conversation:

1. What behavior has the coachee committed to complete before our next session?

2. When the coachee implements their plan, will they be closer to their goal?

3. How will we know? What is the external objective measure?

One way coaches can answer those three questions is to use the well-known SMART mnemonic for creating a "smart" plan.

CREATING A SMART PLAN

A SMART plan is Specific, Measurable, Action-oriented, Realistic, and Timely. Coaches can either explain the SMART acronym or simply keep it as a mental checklist while those they coach create their plans.

Specific—Being specific means all terms are defined and agreed to. People who develop a specific plan are more likely to complete it because it contains a concrete goal. It is not vague.

Example: *"Get more exercise by walking three miles a day at least five days out of seven,"* not *"get more exercise."*

Measurable—The plan should contain an external observable measure. This ensures the expected behavior is clear, and it eliminates any argument about whether the plan was completed. When the plan is measurable, the coachee can self-evaluate. They either completed the plan or they did not.

Example: *"Be at work with computer and headset on by 8:00 a.m.,"* not *"be at work on time."*

Action-oriented—Coaching is about completing effective behaviors. The plan must include an action. An action-oriented plan lets the coachee answer the Doing question in their next coaching conversation.

Example: *"Complete three calls per day to existing customers,"* not *"improve customer service."*

Realistic—The plan needs to be something the coachee has a good chance of completing.

Example: *"I will be at work on time (see Measurable) for the next ten days,"* not *"I will never be late again."*

Timely—A typical coaching cycle includes contact with a coach every one or two weeks. The plan should contain actions that can be completed during one coaching cycle.

Example: refer to examples for Action-oriented (three calls per day) and Realistic (ten days).

Every plan does not have to be a SMART plan. But these five words provide an easy checklist for coaches as the coachee creates a plan. If some parts are not clear or are missing, coaches can ask questions to help clarify the plan. It may be helpful to share the mnemonic with the person being coached, when a coach thinks that would help.

GOLD STARS, CARROTS AND STICKS

Coaching is not manipulation. It is a straightforward process to help achieve something. We define manipulation as anything that would lose its power or effectiveness if you knew what we were doing. For instance, a salesperson may try to convince you to buy something you may not want by using an "assumptive close." They act as if you have already decided to buy. *"Do you want the red one or the blue one?"* The salesperson may call it "persuasion." We call it manipulation that attempts to make it more difficult for the buyer to say "no." Manipulation relies on external control. It is the opposite of allowing free choice and internal control.

Coaches help coachees realize they have choices and they are responsible for their own thoughts and actions. This is a big insight for people who have been controlled externally most of their lives. External control is the predominant approach used by many, including parents and managers, to get people to do things. Some people have only known this approach: carrot and stick, reward and punish, Do To and Do For (fear and guilt), A and F grades. These people experience a major reality shift when coaches explain to them that since they are the only person who can choose their behavior, it just makes sense they should decide what behavior to enact.

With a little practice, when coaches hear a story, they can tell immediately if the storyteller is addicted to external control. The story will be some version of, *"This happened to me and then this happened to me so what else could I do? I had to do what I did. I had no choice."* The story is all about what happened to the person, as if they were only bystanders in their own life. We have previously mentioned coaches should listen for and not accept excuses. The coach's "excuse alarm" should go off when they hear statements like *"There's nothing I can do"* or *"I've tried everything."*

For example:

> *"The traffic was a nightmare, so I got to work late. My stupid boss had scheduled a meeting to start first thing, so the traffic made me late to the meeting. When I got there my boss made a big point about the importance of timeliness. Like it was my fault! Well, of course his comment made me mad for the rest of the day. When I got home my wife asked how my day went. I'm human so I yelled at her. It was a horrible day. My work is driving me nuts."*

One term for this explanatory style is victim thinking. Dr. Stephen Covey, the self-help author, referred to this explanatory style as *reactive* thinking. A reactive thinker describes their behavior as if something external caused their behavior. The stimulus caused the response. There were no other choices and it was not the person's fault. They were the victim.

Covey called the opposite of this way of thinking *proactive* thinking. In that case, a person receives a stimulus with their five senses, considers their options based on their internal world, chooses a response, and then acts. The idea that people choose their responses to what happens to them is the basis for Glasser's Choice Theory and is fundamental to our approach to coaching.

85

When we hear one of those *"The dog ate my homework"* stories, we often say, *"Okay, tell that story again with you in it."*

Then the person might say:

"I knew I had an early meeting at work, and I set my alarm to go off earlier. Apparently, I still underestimated the traffic because I arrived late to work and to the meeting. When I got there my boss referred to our company values on the wall, one of which is timeliness. I apologized, but I still felt bad about it. I tried to salvage the rest of the day but it wasn't a great day for me. When I got home my wife, meaning well, asked how my day went. I told her I arrived late and felt late all day, but now it's over and I was glad to be home. Some days work really seems like work."

One of the rewards of coaching is helping people learn to regain more internal control in their lives by becoming aware of and changing their explanatory style to tell better stories. As a result, their lives become more "want to" and less "have to."

> **Achieving different results means either changing what you want or how you behave.**

We have taken a closer look at the four basic coaching questions. They are like the individual steps to a dance. Now let's see how to put them together into coaching conversations. Let's dance.

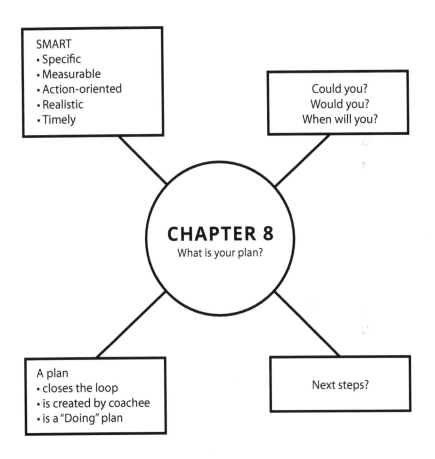

SECTION 3

PUTTING THE QUESTIONS INTO PRACTICE

Putting the Questions into Practice

The four coaching questions are at the heart of the coaching process. But *using* the questions to help people is the whole reason for learning them. This third section of the book helps coaches plan for and conduct coaching conversations, troubleshoot issues that arise, and apply the coaching concepts in broader ways.

9

BEFORE THE FIRST CONVERSATION

"You hit home runs not by chance but
by preparation."

—Roger Maris, American professional baseball player

Coaches can use the four coaching questions, WDIP, in a number of ways. Some coaching conversations happen spontaneously. Other situations require a more deliberate approach. Before coaches begin any serious coaching process, they need to do a little planning.

OVERCOME YOUR RESISTANCE TO COACHING

We have talked about the internal stories people tell themselves—the self-talk that either supports or sabotages their behavior and results. Coaches need to recognize their own biases and tell themselves helpful stories about their coaching. Coaches who use a behavioral style assessment like the DISC will find it helpful to take stock of their own behavioral preferences. Otherwise, coaches need to be good observers of themselves and need to ask others they trust for feedback about their behavior.

For instance, coaches with a results-driven, fast-paced and extroverted behavioral style may tend to tell themselves they "don't have time" to coach. Or, as one of our clients once said, *"I don't want to coach. I want to fire."* A more helpful story could be, *"If I invest time in coaching this person now, I will save time in the long run."*

Coaches who are extroverted and more people-focused than results-focused enjoy interacting with others and fear any type of social rejection. They may avoid coaching by telling themselves, *"People won't like me if I coach them."* A more helpful story for this type of coach could be, *"If I coach people and they get themselves back on track, they will like and trust me in the future."*

Coaches who are introverted, people-focused, and good listeners usually do not like surprises or a fast-paced environment. They tend to accommodate problems rather than confront them. These coaches may tell themselves, *"The problem is not that bad. It will probably work itself out."* A more helpful story may be, *"Coaching is about listening and I am a good listener. I can listen to others and help them be more effective."*

Coaches whose style is introverted and task-focused may not like criticism of their work. Their coaching story could be, *"I don't know enough to coach. I don't want to goof up."* A better story could be, *"I know the basics of coaching. It is not that hard. If I want to become a better coach I just need to start coaching and learn from my experience."*

Coaches need to listen to their own stories and make sure they are telling helpful ones.

DEVELOP RULES OF ENGAGEMENT

The term Rules of Engagement (ROE) refers to a list of military dos and don'ts for a given situation. They spell out how much force is acceptable and typically list what can and cannot be done in a particular situation. We borrowed that military term to describe a list of dos and don'ts for the relationship between a coach, the person being coached, and any others involved.

The ROE establishes the ground rules for everyone involved in the coaching process. It sets the tone for the relationship as fair, open, and win-win. It establishes a Do With environment. Every coach should create a list of dos and don'ts and discuss it with the others involved in any formal coaching situation. Exactly what goes on the list and who needs to be involved will vary depending on the situation.

As an example, let's suppose a company wants to hire you as a coach to work with one of their executives. In this case, you would discuss the ROE with whomever is contracting with you before you accept the engagement. You would also discuss the ROE with the executive you will be coaching and modify it if needed. The idea is the ROE can be modified or amended, but it cannot be violated.

In this case—with you being asked to come in to a company and work with an executive—you might want to discuss the following with the person who is hiring you. The decisions reached about these topics would go in the ROE.

- Verify the coachee has been specifically told by their management why they are being coached.

- Ensure the coachee is clearly aware of the consequences of not changing their behavior.

- Define the coachee's behavior (using observable facts) that is the cause for this coaching.

- Estimate the hard and soft costs to the company of this coachee's present behavior.

- Agree on the price and payments for this engagement.

- List any other facts and data (not assumptions and conclusions) related to this coaching.

- Document desired outcomes for all parties. Describe the best outcomes possible.

- Define the estimated length of this coaching relationship and how often coach and coachee will meet.

- Decide who can terminate the coaching relationship. For example, the engagement may be stopped by the coach at any time and by the coachee any time after four weeks.

- Determine how the coach may access the coachee's manager, peers, and direct reports.
- Verify the goal is for the coach and the coachee to attempt to resolve any disagreements themselves before involving others.
- List any boundaries, rules, procedures, laws, or social norms that are being violated by the coachee.
- List topics, if any, that are off-limits for the coach.

This list is an example of the information you may need to gather to create an ROE. You may want to add items to an ROE as a result of something unexpected that happened in a previous coaching session. The idea is to explicitly state, before the fact, any results, guidelines, and expectations that are important to the success of the coaching relationship along with any conditions where someone can "run out of bounds." The ROE is a great way to head off misunderstandings before they occur.

KNOW THE PURPOSE OF THE COACHING SESSION

A coach must be clear about the purpose of any coaching session. Coaching is about helping people use more effective behaviors. Coaches should always ask themselves these questions:

- What is the main issue or purpose of this next session?

- What behavior change do I need to focus on with the person I am coaching?

- Will the person I am coaching agree that the change is needed?

- Is there more than one issue that needs focus?

- What is the stated root cause that created this coaching opportunity?

DECIDE WHOSE SCALES ARE OUT OF BALANCE

We used the metaphor of the balance scale in Chapter 7 to describe the difference between what someone wants and what they perceive they are getting. The coach needs to know, for any coaching situation, whose scales are out of balance. The person being coached? The person contracting the coach? The coach? Others involved? Other people may or may not be affected, but until people being coached feel an imbalance in their scales, they will be reluctant to choose different behaviors.

The best situation for a coach is when the coachee's scales are out of balance and they are open to changing their behavior. If, while developing the ROE, the coach believes someone else's scales are out of balance, the coach should deal with that situation before proceeding. For instance, an employee's manager may be reluctant to give the employee honest feedback and instead chooses to employ a coach. The coach can choose to accept the assignment or, if the manager is open to it, the coach could help the manager get more comfortable giving feedback. Each situation is different. We are suggesting that, as part of the preparation, a coach needs to clarify who is not getting what they want and why.

CONSIDER PERSONAL MOTIVATORS AND BEHAVIORAL STYLES

We discussed the coachee's personal motivation in conjunction with the Want question and different behavioral styles in conjunction with the Doing question. We reviewed the idea of different behavioral styles of coaches earlier in this chapter. Before having the first conversation, coaches need to think about their own personal motivators and behavioral traits as well as those of the people they are coaching.

Coaches should do what they can to minimize their own behavioral and motivational biases. For example, coaches who tend to avoid confrontation may want to be a bit more direct. Coaches who tend to "tell it like it is" may want to be less direct. Coaches who tend to lecture need to listen more and talk less. Coaches may need to seek feedback from a variety of people to get a clear picture of their impact on others.

Coaches should also think about who they are working with and adapt their conversational style to communicate in a way that is helpful to the person being coached. For example, when coaching people who display an introverted and task-based behavioral style, coaches will want to focus on providing a "safety net" by giving those coached more time than usual to evaluate their situations. Coaches who modify their communication styles to mesh with the people they are coaching usually get rewarded with a quicker, higher-quality, more effective coaching experience.

It is likely the coach and the person being coached will have different motivators—the internal drivers that influence what a person wants. This is one more reason why RealTime Coaching counsels coaches to not judge or criticize. All people judge from their own frame of reference or values. For example, a coach may be motivated by a high return on investment. They may be coaching a person who is indifferent to getting a return on their investment of time and resources. The coachee may be motivated by altruism. In that case the coachee will be focused on helping others, not on the bottom line. The coach will not be successful if they try to focus on the bottom line instead of on helping others. Coaches who understand and adapt to the personal motivators and behavioral style of the people they are coaching will improve their conversations and results.

As competent coaches listen to those they are coaching, they are on the lookout for "motivational stressors" or mismatches as possible causes for problems. For instance, if the coachee mentioned above (with the low regard for return on investment and a high desire to help others) is in a sales job where they must make a quota—the more they sell the more they make—and they are told to do whatever it takes to make that sale (let the buyer beware), you can bet an internal motivational mismatch will result in external performance issues. Coachees who become aware of this type of mismatch may have an "aha" moment where insight and progress can occur.

USE EFFECTIVE OPENING LINES

Coaches who have spent a little time preparing for the first coaching conversation will have thought about the behavioral style of the person they are coaching. The coach should consider that style, then craft an approach that will have a positive impact on the coachee.

Of course, each conversation will vary depending not only on the motivators and behavioral styles of those involved but also the history, the state of the relationship, severity of the issue and many other variables. As a general rule, we recommend that coaches be straightforward and clear about the purpose of the conversations. Get it on the table quickly. What a coach does *not* want is for the coachee to be sitting there thinking, *"Why am I here? What is this about?"*

A coachee who is extroverted and task oriented will prefer that the coach be direct while remaining respectful and get right to it.

> **Coach/Manager:** *Thanks for coming in, Frank. I want to talk to you about a work issue.*

If a coach uses that same opening statement with a person who is more people-focused and less results-focused, without at least a little personal chitchat first, the coach will come across as cold. The same statement to a more introverted coachee will be even more threatening and may quickly put the person on the defensive.

Thinking about the right approach should not be manipulative. We have said nothing, nor will we ever, about trying to fool the person being coached. Coaching is a bit like having a conversation with someone who does not speak your native language. If you know that other person's language, it makes sense to use it. It is respectful and leads to better results. Put some thought into how a conversation should begin while remaining mindful of the purpose of the conversation. Keep the Platinum Rule in mind: *"Treat others the way they want to be treated."*

PREPARE A FEW WDIP QUESTIONS BEFOREHAND

No one can plan a conversation exactly as it will unfold. However, well-prepared coaches take the time to jot down a few questions representing each of the four WDIP coaching questions as a way to start their conversations in the desired direction and on a positive note.

USE A PRACTICE PARTNER

For new coaches or those who need more preparation for an upcoming conversation, we recommend using a practice partner to help prepare for the actual conversation. The partner takes the role of the person to be coached. The coach can give the partner as much or as little background as they think appropriate. Then they have one or more conversations. Of course, the real conversation will be different. However, the coach will almost always gain insights from the practice that will improve the actual conversation.

When we offer coaching workshops within an organization, people who participate can become excellent practice partners for others in the workshop. They understand coaching and they are usually familiar with the culture and context. If coaches do not have this pool of partners to choose from, they can find someone who has a general understanding of the situation. They can then give their partner a short tutorial on the concept of coaching along with background information about the upcoming conversation.

World-class performers in any field spend an enormous amount of time practicing and improving. In fact, that time is much greater than the amount of time they spend performing. To become an effective coach, invest in practice and preparation. It is time well spent.

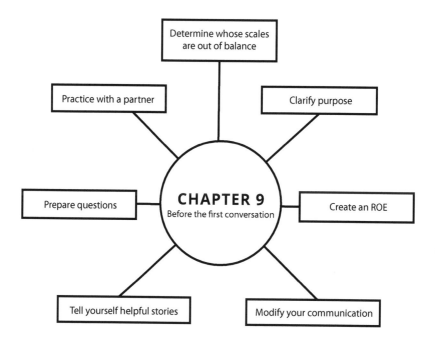

10

THE FIRST CONVERSATION

"Can we talk?"

—Joan Rivers, American comedian

BUILD RELATIONSHIPS TO CREATE RESULTS

The ability of coaches to positively influence other people depends in part on how the other people perceive the coach. Coaches work with a whole spectrum of relationships. They may find themselves coaching someone they barely know, someone they don't particularly like, or one of their best friends. Coaching is an opportunity to *increase* the amount of trust in any relationship. Effective coaches approach every coaching conversation with a heart at peace, not a heart at war, and with win-win intentions.

When someone is experiencing difficulty in their life, a problematic relationship is often the root cause. This may not be evident right away, but will emerge over the course of the coaching sessions. Coaches can help with that difficult relationship by first creating a Do With relationship with the person they are coaching. The coaching relationship may be the only win-win relationship in the person's life at the time. An adult-to-adult relationship not only helps a coach be more effective and helps the person being coached to be self-accountable; it also gives the person being coached an actual model of how a positive relationship can work. At the heart of any healthy relationship is a balance of courage to speak up and compassion to listen.

Coaches focus on their words, body language, and pace of speech. What they say and how they say it should improve the quality and the amount of trust in the relationship. A coach's communication style should make communication easier for the person being coached.

KNOW YOUR INTENTION

Goal, aim, and *purpose* are all synonyms for the word *intention.* In the last chapter, we mentioned the need to think about your coaching intention as a part of preparing to coach. It is also important for coaches to keep their coaching intention in mind as they begin any coaching conversation. This is critical to becoming an effective coach.

We used Lewis Carroll's quote, *"If you don't know where you are going, any road will take you there."* to introduce chapter

8. It also applies here. To go down the right road, competent coaches are always aware of their intentions. They can answer the following questions:

1. What is my intention for this conversation? Why am I having this conversation?

2. What specifically do I want to accomplish?

3. How will this conversation support the person I am coaching?

The answers to these questions should be focused and helpful to all parties. For instance,

1. My purpose during this conversation is to help Sam with time management and establishing priorities.

2. I want to help Sam make and take ownership of a SMART plan to be at work on time.

3. Sam requested my help. I will do my best to support his desire to get to work on time.

A coach with a pure intention and a basic understanding of the four coaching questions can be more effective than a coach who has more "coaching tricks" but lacks a positive intention.

Coaches also need to consider the long-term outcomes of their intentions.

- Who do I want to be as a coach?
- What do I need to do to be this coach?
- How do I want to be remembered as a coach?

If you have gotten this far in the book, you may recognize this thinly disguised set of WDIP questions, minus the Is question that coaches can use on themselves. These questions are not just answered once and then forgotten. The coach continually uses them to self-evaluate and become more effective as they work with others.

LISTEN

During coaching conversations, coaches should listen much more than they talk. Coaches have a general direction for a session in mind but do not force the conversation. Because coaches ask questions for the benefit of those they coach, the answers to those questions will determine the specific direction the conversation takes.

Listening is a great way to demonstrate interest in and respect for another person. Once people feel understood, they are ready to work on solutions. The coach's time during a conversation should mostly be spent listening, then asking questions. The least amount of time should be spent lecturing or making statements.

Genuine listening, from the perspective of "seeing how they see it, feeling how they feel it," will build trust in any relationship. Coaches listen to understand the other person's thinking. The responses of the person being coached often shine a light on that person's motivations and reasons for their behavior. This deepens the coach's understanding of their actions.

Personal motivators are normally invisible to a coach or any other person.

In addition, listening provides a quiet place where people can reflect on their issues and allow new ideas to surface. Coaches need to be comfortable with silence when it happens. Remaining silent will take some practice for most people, especially extroverted coaches who enjoy talking. These coaches are also likely to underestimate the amount of time they are actually talking. Competent coaches don't break the silence by offering ideas for what to do next.

> **Listen to understand the other person.**
> **See it as they see it. Feel it as they feel it.**

STAY FOCUSED

At times, coaches will be working with people who have been asked to change their behavior by their employer or family or someone else. These people may not particularly want to be coached, or want to change. In these cases, the scales of the people being coached are in balance but the scales of those requesting the coaching are not in balance. We will discuss this subject more later in the book (see When Coaching Doesn't Work). For now, we want to remind coaches that, for the conversation to move forward, it is important to stay focused. Here are some common signs of a coachee's desire to deflect the direction of the conversation:

1. *"My previous managers never made me do this."*

2. *"The last person I rented from wasn't as picky as you are."*

3. *"Other people in the department do it too. Why don't you talk to them?"*

4. *"Tell me who complained about me. It was Mary, wasn't it?"*

5. *"Nobody's perfect. What about all the good things I do?"*

Choose to see these kinds of statements as helpful signs. It means the people being coached are being encouraged to take personal responsibility and change behaviors, even if they are reluctant to do so. The coach's answers to the above statements need to keep the conversation on track without getting hooked into a side conversation. Some possible responses are:

1. *"Well, maybe not. But now I am your manager."* Or, *"Yes, times have changed."*

2. *"Are you saying you want to go back to your last apartment?"*

3. *"I may talk to other people, but right now I want to talk with you."*

4. *"It really doesn't matter who is complaining, or if anyone is complaining. I'd like us to talk about an issue that is affecting your performance. Are you willing to do that?"*

5. *"Yes, you do some things very well. And yes, everyone has flaws. This flaw is affecting your performance. Are you interested in improving your performance?"*

Of course, there are many ways to answer those questions. Coaches need to use language they are comfortable with, language that is authentic for them. Just try to acknowledge the other person's comment without losing track of the main focus of the conversation, and without reverting to a Do To or a Do For approach.

ASK GOOD QUESTIONS

All coaching questions are not equal. A good question is one that matters. A coach asks a good question because they want to know the answer, not just because it is in a list of possible questions. Good questions are relatively unbiased, free of opinions and personality. Good coaching questions result in learning and perhaps an "aha" moment because they encourage thinking as well as action. Good questions can help people being coached become aware of their reality—their thinking, behavior, and results—in a new way. And when their view of reality changes, they will more easily choose different and more appropriate behaviors to get what they want.

END WITH A PLAN

In this respect, the first conversation is no different than all those that follow. Each coaching conversation is not complete until a specific plan has been developed. The *coachee* develops the plan with the help of the coach. The plan should keep the process moving forward at an appropriate pace with specific action items to be completed by the coachee between conversations. A plan is the one item that will keep a coaching conversation on track and headed toward a successful conclusion. A plan spells out the specific work that is expected to be done before the next coaching session. Without this, progress will stall and frustrations will rise. Review chapter 8 on the Plan question for reminders about what makes a good plan.

Ending with a plan also applies to coaches. Sometimes during coaching, something will remind the coach of an article or book that might be helpful, and the coach will probably mention it to the coachee. After the conversation, the coach needs to follow through and obtain the item, if possible. This applies for any type of commitment or promise made by coaches. If one of the goals of coaching is to build and model a trusting win-win relationship, then keeping promises and following through on commitments are crucial behaviors for coaches as well as the people they coach.

> **A successful first coaching conversation moves the coachee closer to their goal.**

PRACTICING INFORMAL COACHING

Coaching does not always have to be a formal conversation. Once someone gets accustomed to coaching, they will find many opportunities to informally coach, ranging from conversations with coworkers to passing conversations with a stranger in the airport.

Let's listen to a conversation between Eric and Informal Coach (who is a peer of Eric's), as they walk to the weekly staff meeting:

> **Eric:** *I don't look forward to these meetings. It seems like the only reason for the meeting is that it's Monday morning.*
>
> **IC:** *That's the way it seems sometimes. Plus, I have a bunch of deadlines looming. I wonder what we could do to make these meetings more useful for us?*

And so the informal conversation begins, with a gentle Plan question. Maybe it results in some changes to the meeting. Maybe it doesn't. It does create the possibility that a more productive and interesting conversation can occur, and it minimizes the gripe session. It gently and subtly turns the conversation into a "what can we do" brainstorming session.

As coaches gain experience, they move from only coaching in "special" conversations to using their coaching skills as a part of who they are. Said another way, coaching is not just for "fixing problems." If coaching is only used when there is a problem, people will quickly come to associate coaching with being reprimanded. Nothing could be further from what we intend. Coaching can, and should, also be used for positively supporting people.

To avoid falling into the trap of only using coaching for negative situations, see coaching as a skill that can be practiced and developed when working with others. Coaching can be appropriate for use during the first conversation of a high performer, during the last conversation with a "problem child" who is moving on and at many points in between.

Coaching is not just for fixing problems.

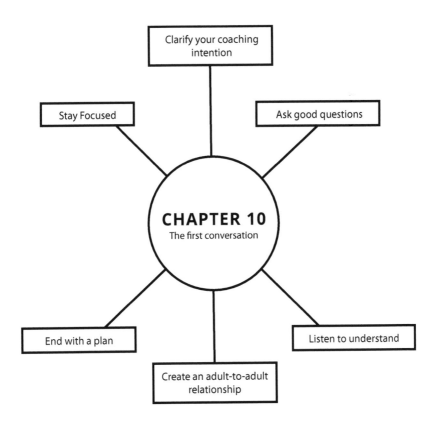

11 COACHING BEYOND THE FIRST CONVERSATION

"As a human being I am work in process."

—John Lydon (aka Johnny Rotten), English musician

Sometimes having one coaching conversation with a person will be all that is required. For most situations, however, more than one conversation will be needed. Coaching is a process, and each conversation is one cycle of the process. A typical coaching process takes place over a number of conversations, often lasting weeks or months. This is particularly true if the person being coached is making a major change or a number of changes.

Each coaching conversation is a step along the path toward success. Coaches help people become accountable for their progress by

- Making sure each conversation ends with a concrete, workable plan.

- Beginning each subsequent conversation with a review of the progress made on the previous plan.

- Celebrating successes and not accepting excuses.

- Knowing when to correct the course to keep the process moving toward a resolution rather than stalling out.

START THE FOLLOW-ON CONVERSATION

Follow-on coaching conversations help people make changes and advance in the direction they have chosen. How these conversations begin goes a long way toward setting the right tone for the session. Before each session, coaches should be clear about what they want to accomplish. Then they can use the opening questions to set the stage for that result. Following are a few possible questions:

- How was your week?

- What has happened since our last meeting?

- Did anything happen this past week that you would like to discuss?

- Would you say things are better, worse, or about the same?

- What would you like to accomplish today?

- Where would you like to start today?

- How did your plan from our last conversation work out?

In addition to getting the session started in the right direction, these questions subtly remind the coachee that this is their process and the coach is their accountability partner.

REVIEW THE PLAN

You can see from those questions that the agreed-to plan created at the last coaching session is the usual starting point for the follow-up session. If the person being coached completed the plan and thinks it helped, the conversation moves forward from there. *"Good job. What's next?"* If they did not complete the plan or did not think it helped, the session starts there. In either case the coach should congratulate the coachee on work completed and accept no excuses for work not completed.

With a well-crafted SMART plan (as described in Chapter 8), it should be easy for both the coach and the coachee to determine whether the plan was completed. In this way coaches help people be accountable for working toward what they want to achieve without wasting either the coach's or the coachee's time. Without plans, coaching conversations will likely get off-track by rehashing old issues, disagreeing about what the coachee was supposed to do, or with the coachee restating excuses.

CREATE A POSITIVE RELATIONSHIP

It is not an overstatement to say the quality of the coaching process can be no better than the quality of the coach/

coachee relationship. It should be a positive relationship based on mutual trust and mutual respect. If you have read this far, you understand that coaching requires the person being coached to be accountable for their own thoughts and actions. Coaches support progress, help those they coach be accountable and model responsible behavior.

> **A quality coaching relationship is built on mutual trust and mutual respect.**

Following is a typical follow-on coaching conversation between an employee who has a habit of not getting to work on time and a coach from outside the company. We will eliminate a lot of the small talk and chitchat, but notice how the coach is treating the coachee with respect and maturity while keeping the conversation on track.

Coach: *Welcome back. How was your week?*

Coachee: *It was okay. How was yours?*

Coach: *I had a good week. Thanks for asking. Last week we ended our conversation with a plan. As I recall you were going to be at work with your headphones and computer on every day by or before 8:00 a.m. Am I remembering that correctly?*

Coachee: *Yes.*

Coach: *Did you complete that plan?*

Coachee: *Almost. I was on time for the first four days. I was a little late on Friday—really bad traffic.*

A coach gives credit where it is due while helping the person be accountable for their plan. A coach does not demean or belittle the person being coached as this would harm a relationship built on mutual respect.

> **Coach:** *It's good that you got to work on time the first four days. But that was not the whole plan, right?*
>
> **Coachee:** *Right.*
>
> **Coach:** *Are you concerned about what will happen to you if you only get to work on time 80 percent of the time?*
>
> **Coachee:** *Do you think they will fire me?*
>
> **Coach:** *I can't speak for your employer. Sounds like you are concerned about it.*
>
> **Coachee:** *Of course I'm concerned! I don't want to lose my job.*
>
> **Coach:** *What do you want?*
>
> **Coachee:** *I want to keep my job. I'd also like to earn more money.*

A coach helps the person focus on the reality of the external world.

> **Coach:** *I doubt they are going to raise your salary if you can't get there on time.*

Coachee: *I have to agree with you there.*

The coach wants to see if this person will take responsibility for his or her behavior.

Coach: *So who was responsible for your late arrival Friday?*

Coachee: *I told you. It was horrible traffic.*

Coach: *It was the traffic's fault? Were most people late on Friday?*

Coachee: *Not really. (pause) I see what you're saying. You're back on that kick about me being responsible.*

Coach: *Yes. What are you responsible for?*

Coachee: *My thoughts and actions.*

Coach: *If you really believe that, who was responsible for your late arrival at work?*

Coachee: *I guess I was, but sometimes things just happen.*

Coach senses this person has not really accepted the idea of self-responsibility and is just telling the coach what they want to hear. Coach decides to "unbalance the scales" of this person, to encourage a change of thinking and behavior.

Coach: *Until you decide you're the only person who can get you to work on time, I'm not sure there's much more we can do here. We might as well stop meeting.*

Coachee: *If my boss finds out you won't see me, I'll be in bigger trouble.*

Coach: *Look, I'm not trying to get you in trouble. I actually like working with you, but I don't want to waste your time and your company's money unless I think we can make progress. As long as you're willing to blame not getting to work on time on anything other than yourself, ethically I don't feel like I should keep seeing you.*

Coachee: *Okay, if you're going to make me...*

Coach: *Hold it. Don't even finish that sentence. I can't make you do anything. That is just what we have been talking about. You choose your behavior. Maybe you like goofing off in the morning. Maybe you have never had to be on a schedule. I don't know, and it's not even important because that's all in the past. It's over. Let's focus on the present and near future. You have a lot of control over that. Moving forward for this next week, what do you want to do with regard to getting to work on time?*

Coachee: *This next week I'll be at work every day on time, with my computer and headphones on, before 8:00 a.m.*

Coach: *Okay. Do you have some ideas about how you are going to keep from repeating last week's performance?*

Coachee: *Yes. I think so. I need my job. I'll do better.*

Coach: *Do you want to talk about your strategies for this next week?*

Coachee: *No.*

Coach: *Okay. I have one more question. I know there is some small chance for something outside your control to occur that would cause you to be late for work—a big accident for instance. As you say, "Things happen." Barring some major incident outside of your control, what do you think you and I should do if you are late for work even one day this next week?*

Coachee: *What do you mean?*

Coach: *Behaviors have natural consequences—results. When you choose the behavior, you choose the consequences. As the old saying goes, "If you can't do the time, don't do the crime." I'm not saying it's a crime to be late for work, but what do you think are the natural consequences?*

Coachee: *After last week, I'm on probation at work. I guess they could fire me.*

Coach: *Thinking about it in the way we discussed—you being responsible—would it really be "them" who fired you?*

Coachee: (Long pause, thinking) *I would be firing myself by coming in late?*

Coach thinks, *"Hmm, maybe we have a chance here."*

Coach: *Right. Exactly. And what do you think the consequences will be with me?*

Coachee: *After what you said, you might quit seeing me.*

Coach: *And what are the consequences for your wife and family?*

Coachee: *I'm the bread winner. I would be letting my family down.*

Coach: *In light of these natural consequences, what will you choose to do this next week with regard to getting to work on time?*

Coachee: *I'm going to be on time—maybe even a little early—every day.*

Coach: *Great. I have confidence that you can do this if you keep in mind what we've talked about. You are the owner of your behavior. Because of that, you own the consequences of your behavior. If you need to talk to me during the week, feel free to call any time. I'll look forward to seeing you next week.*

USE DATA

During the coaching process, coaches rely on facts and data rather than conclusions and judgment. Coaches can obtain facts and data: (1) from the person being coached, (2) from the coach's own observations, (3) from other interested people, such as coworkers, bosses, and spouses, and (4) from objective data such as quality and quantity measures, or time arrived at work.

The *person being coached* may have evidence indicating what they need to do to be more effective. They are the ones most familiar with their situation. For example, our coachee who is often late to work knows they have been staying up late at night to finish a project, making it more difficult to get up the following morning. Do not let them confuse facts with excuses, such as blaming outside forces (traffic) for their own problems. Do be open to what they are saying. Listen for what they are and are not aware of (what they might be blind to).

Coaches can help those they coach create facts and data through the use of the, *"On a scale of one to ten . . ."* question we have mentioned before. For example, in the conversation about getting to work on time, this could happen:

> **Coach:** *You said getting to work on time was important for you.*
>
> **Coachee:** *Yes.*
>
> **Coach:** *On a scale of one to ten, one being not important and ten being most important, how important is it for you to get to work on time?*
>
> **Coachee:** *I'd say about an eight. Yeah, seven or eight.*
>
> **Coach:** *What is more important than that? Do you have any nines or tens in your life?*
>
> **Coachee:** *My wife and kids. I love 'em. They are a ten.*
>
> **Coach:** *What happens to your family if you lose your job?*
>
> **Coachee:** *I see what you mean. Maybe work is a nine.*

A *coach* will naturally have their own view of what the coachee needs to do to improve. The coach is in a perfect position to listen to the coachee and make observations. However, everyone has biases and blind spots. The coach must be willing to separate their observations from their conclusions. Coaches need to remain nonjudgmental and in control of their emotions. They should use this source of data carefully and sparingly. Make as few assumptions as possible.

A coach can ask *others'* opinions of the performance of the person being coached. The coach needs to do this in a way the people being questioned know the information will be used to help the coachee—for development, not discipline—and will be kept confidential. The level of trust in the culture will determine how beneficial this data is.

A coach can look at *measures of performance* such as quality and quantity of work, timeliness (at work by 8:00 a.m.), customer service measures, and others to see what these measures say about the coachee's performance. Every person deserves to have objective measures of success for their job.

GIVE REAL-TIME FEEDBACK

Coaches can often learn a lot by observing how the people they are coaching act during the coaching session. People can be unaware of their behaviors and the impact of these behaviors on others. Coaches can observe and discuss behaviors they see during a session, giving real-time feedback. For example:

Coach: *One thing I hear from the people who work with you is that you tend to try to control every situation.*

Coachee: *I've heard that, too. I think it used to be true, but I've worked on it so I don't think it's a problem any more. I probably don't take enough control.*

Coach: *You don't take enough control?*

Coachee: *Right. Sometimes, anyway. Look, I don't think this is an issue so why don't we move on?*

Coach: *Okay, but before we do I have a conclusion I'd like to share with you. This is my conclusion so it may be right or wrong. It feels like you are trying to control me right now.*

Coachee: *No, I'm not. I just don't want to waste time on this.*

Coach: *Well, when you push to change the subject, it feels to me like you're being controlling. Maybe other people experience this same feeling, too. Is that what you want?*

(Note the coach takes responsibility for the coach's feeling and conclusion and checks it out, rather than saying, "You are trying to control me now." Then the coach uses a WDIP question to move the conversation back to focus on the coachee.)

When someone being coached exhibits improved behavior that will get them closer to their goal, coaches should authentically give them that feedback in the moment, too.

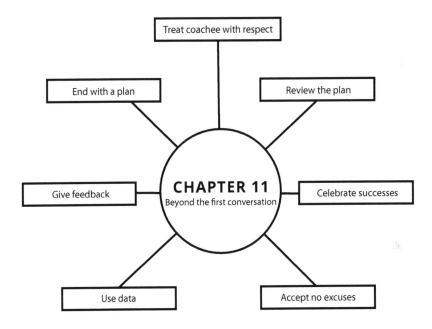

12

WHAT TO DO WHEN COACHING "DOESN'T WORK"

"Experience is what you get when you
didn't get what you wanted."

—Randy Pausch, author of *The Last Lecture*

Like relationships in other parts of life, not every coaching relationship will go smoothly. We and others we know have suc-
cessfully used the theory and practices that make up RealTime
Coaching in a wide range of situations over many years. We
know they work.

And yet, it is not uncommon for us to hear, *"Coaching doesn't
work."* A more accurate statement would be, *"Coaching did not
work for me that time."*

We realize and acknowledge there are times when coaching is not appropriate, and there are people who, for a number of reasons, do not respond to a particular coach. This section provides guidelines for minimizing those situations.

ASSESS THE RELATIONSHIP

At different times, coaches will find themselves working with a stranger, a friend, or someone they do not particularly like. Results flow from relationships, so if a coach thinks they are not being effective with someone, their first step is to estimate the level of trust, respect, and credibility in that relationship.

Coaches may need to improve a relationship to increase their effectiveness. If a coach determines they do not have a positive trusting relationship with someone, they can improve the relationship during the coaching process. People trust trustworthy people, so a coach can follow through on all commitments, make promises sparingly and keep those they make, and keep in confidence anything sensitive said by the coachee.

If someone finds their coach credible and believes their coach has their best interests at heart, and if that coach takes the time to be helpful, then it is more likely that an effective coaching relationship will develop. The act of coaching with the right intention increases the trust in a relationship.

KNOW WHEN NOT TO COACH

There are times when a RealTime Coaching nondirective approach may not be as helpful as a more directive (telling) style.

Examples include:

- When the coach is an expert and the person being coached is a novice. For example, an expert would not explain the operation of a complex machine to a novice by saying, *"How do you think this MRI machine works?"*

- When the situation is hazardous or safety is an issue. A doctor in an emergency room will not be asking, *"Do you know what those defibrillator paddles are used for?"*

- If there is one and only one best way to do something. A surgeon will not ask, *"Think we should scrub first or just dive right in?"*

- When time is short. This requires some self-discipline on the part of coaches, because there never seems to be enough time for anything. In particular, those coaches who are action-and-results-oriented must practice restraint. Even in time-sensitive situations, there is usually time after the crisis to reexamine the situation in a nondirective way. *"On a scale of one to ten, how do you think you performed during the trauma run?"*

Review the particular situation to make sure coaching is an appropriate approach to use.

KNOW WHOM NOT TO COACH

Are there people who cannot be coached? When we get asked this question, we usually respond that there are certainly coach/coachee relationships that do not work. Given the wrong circumstances, anyone can become difficult to coach. We will explore how to diagnose an unsuccessful coaching relationship shortly.

Let's first look at a couple of situations that deserve special comment. We usually have a statement in our Rules of Engagement document to the effect that *"the person being coached is not in need of therapy or other clinical treatment."* We believe it is a mistake and may be unethical to coach someone who needs a more clinical form of assistance. Coaching is not therapy. Coaches need to know where their boundaries are and need to be able to sort out the people who need coaching support from those who need something more.

When evaluating a possible coaching opportunity, coaches should look at two variables: (1) how egregious the unwanted behavior is, and (2) how often it occurs. If the behavior is not "way out of bounds" and/or it occurs infrequently, the situation more easily lends itself to coaching. People who are often exhibiting extreme behavior may need to be dealt with in a different way, particularly if the behavior does not improve after a conversation or two.

CHECK FOR BALANCE AND FIND MUTUAL PURPOSE

As a coach, when you are assessing an upcoming coaching situation, use the metaphor of the balance scale. Remember the scale represents what a person *wants* on one side, and on the other side what the person *perceives they are getting at the time*. When a person's scale is in balance, they are getting what they want and are motivated to continue their present behavior. If a person's scale is out of balance, they will be motivated to change behavior to get what they want.

Coaching is effective when someone's scale is out of balance. If a person is not happy with the results they perceive they are getting, they are usually receptive to getting help and support from a coach whose intention is to help them get what they want. This is obviously a coaching opportunity.

However, if a coach's scale is out of balance, it means the coach wants a different result from what the coachee wants. For example, if the coach is in a supervisory or managerial position, their scale may be out of balance because they want someone else to do something differently. In that case, the other person needs to change their behavior, but that person's scale is likely in balance and they see no need to change.

A basic principle of RealTime Coaching is people choose their behavior. Early in this book we talked about three different ways to influence others: Do To, Do For, and Do With. Although Do To can certainly unbalance another person's scale using fear, "Do this or else" is not coaching. It is coercion. Do For can also unbalance scales by using guilt or shame. Neither of these influence approaches works well in the long term. Nor are they what we consider to be coaching.

The Do With approach requires that there is something the coach and the coachee will do together (Do With each other). Therefore, the coach and the person being coached must first find a mutual purpose—something they both care about. That shared purpose becomes the Want in the coaching model. Once there is agreement on this want, or goal, or desire, then the conversation can turn to the Doing behaviors.

Behaviors are peoples' strategies to get what they want. There are usually a number of strategies that will achieve a given purpose. During these conversations, it is not unusual for a new and different strategy or set of acceptable behaviors to emerge. Coaches need to be open to new approaches and solutions while not wavering on the purpose. For example, the basic ideas in the following conversation occurred during one of our workshops:

> **Manager/Coach (MC):** *You need to shift your work hours next week to come in an hour later and stay an hour later to cover the phones in case we get calls from our customers. The company is making this change to provide better customer service. We will rotate this role through the department, so you will only have to do this a couple weeks a month, at most.*

Employee: *That's really a problem for me. My wife and I have this tight schedule. I get home just in time to watch the kids so she can leave for her job. Can't someone else stay over and answer the phones?*

MC: *This new work is a bit of a problem for everyone. So I can't ask the others to stay over and let you go home. Everybody in the department needs to take their turn.*

Employee: *Are you saying you are going to fire me if I don't stay over?*

MC: *Let's not get ahead of ourselves. Maybe you and I can find a way to work this out. Let's start with what we both want. I want us to comply with this new corporate request to provide increased customer service.*

Employee: *And I want to get home on time to support my wife and kids. By the way, I want us to give great customer service, too.*

MC: *I know. You are a good soldier. You want to support everybody. I want you to be able to take care of your kids too. And, I certainly don't want to lose you as an employee. If we could find a way to cover the phones and let you get home on time, that would satisfy both of us. Right?*

Employee: *Yes, but how can we do that?*

MC: *Hmm, now that I think about it, is there any reason we cannot have the customer phone forwarded to another number?*

Employee: *Not that I know of. What are you thinking?*

MC: *Could you be available to answer the phone when you are home? If you can answer and respond just the way you would at work, the customer won't even know where you are. You would need to be professional. No barking dogs or crying kids.*

Employee: *Sure, I can do that. Let's give it a try. If it works, great. If there are issues, we'll try something else. I'm sure other department members would also like to use that method.*

MC: *Works for me.*

Employee: *Thanks. I really appreciate this.*

We know not every situation leads to such a happy ending. Our point is it's common for people to have an objective in mind and then lock on the first strategy or solution they think of, and not look any further. *"Here is what we need. And, here is how we do it."*

The Do With approach does not jump to the strategy: the how. First, take time to understand what all parties want. Once this is known, then and only then move to finding strategies that fulfill as much of the combined purpose as possible.

Purpose before strategy. Why before how.

KEEP THE PROCESS ON TRACK

Improvement is ultimately the responsibility of the person being coached. However, when things are not working as planned, use the following checklist to diagnose the problem.

Complete the checklist in the order the items are listed. That is, #1 needs to be addressed before #2. This list is circular. The questions may need to be asked more than once to get to a deeper, more accurate diagnosis. (We acknowledge the book, *Adaptive Coaching: The Art and Practice of a Client-Centered Approach to Performance Improvement* by Terry R. Bacon and Laurie Voss (Nicholas Brealey, 2012), as the basis for the following questions.)

1. Does the person have sufficient awareness of the need for change? Determine this by asking, *"Are you happy with the way things are?"* Or, *"What do you think is going to happen if you continue with your present behavior?"*

2. Does the person feel a strong enough sense of urgency? What will motivate this person to want to make this change? Learning? Money? Power? Faith? Helping others? If a person does not want to change, change is unlikely. To get a sense of the person's urgency, coaches can ask, *"Is this change something you want to do or is it something you think you have to do?"* Or, *"On a scale of one to ten, how important is it for you to change?"*

Coaches can help the people they coach see the change as important. For instance, in the dialog with the person not getting to work on time in the last chapter, the coachee said it was a "seven or eight" on a scale of ten to get to work on time. Although that is not low, the coach helped the person see that being on time was critical to their family's happiness, thus raising it to a nine.

This is a good example of a coach who has identified the coachee's primary personal motivator—taking care of the family. Tying the need to be at work on time to this important basic "want" gives the person being coached more internal motivation to make the change. A person is more likely to change if they see the new behavior will get them something they really value. It will change their view of the new behavior to a "want to." They are less likely to change for any reason that is not as near and dear to them. That kind of change becomes a "have to."

Coaches will also help make the change a priority by being accountability partners. A coach may be one of the few people in the coachee's corner. Therefore, one of the most important things a coach can do is support the person, as well as support the change they are attempting. A coach does this with behavior, not just words. Showing real interest in a person demonstrates support and encouragement.

For example, coaches keep their coaching appointments. They don't cancel or reschedule unless there is an emergency. In that unlikely case, they explain what unforeseen thing happened, apologize and get the next session scheduled as soon as possible. When a coach makes coaching a top priority, the coachee will also make it a top priority.

Although coaches can influence others, they cannot make someone else change who has no interest in changing. As we have said numerous times in this book, people choose their response to what is happening to them. That includes choosing not to change. As Marshall Goldsmith, well-known executive coach, says, *"The time you are wasting in attempting to coach people who don't care is time that is stolen from helping people who do."* Knowing when to quit coaching is often as valuable as knowing how to coach. Just as coaching is done in a respectful manner, stopping the coaching relationship should also be done with respect. That conversation should not diminish the amount of trust in the relationship.

3. Has the person made the decision to change and *expressed that decision*? If not, the coach may need to go back to the previous question about urgency and/or help the coachee *commit* to the change. A coach may say, *"You said you think you want to make this change. Let me ask you, could you make this change?"* If the coachee agrees this change is something they could do, then ask, *"Would you do it?"* If the answer is yes, this leads to the next question—how to do it.

4. Has the person *created* an effective and *specific action plan*? Have they thought about and removed barriers? If not, coaches work with people to create SMART action plans with checkpoints, success measures, and specific next steps to help identify ways to overcome barriers.

5. Has the person started *taking action?* If a person is not taking action, the sense of urgency is not strong enough (want to) or the action plan is not specific enough (how to). Recheck the preceding questions. A coach may say something like, *"You said you wanted to make this change and we created the action plan, but you have not done anything. Are you sure you want to make this change?"* and/or *"Do you have everything you need to begin to make this change?"* To check for sense of urgency, coaches can also ask, *"What is more important to you right now than making this change?"*

6. Has the person received *adequate reinforcement?* Coaches need to provide positive reinforcement when it is warranted, particularly if they are a manager/coach. A statement as simple as, *"Good job, keep up the good work"* can be effective. Positive reinforcement may come from someone else—a department member, someone from another department, a family member, or even an outsider. Coaches may need to nudge the "outsiders" to provide positive reinforcement, as long as it's legitimate. People being coached can also give themselves a little positive reinforcement.

Another way to think about reinforcement is to check the person's ability and motivation. Can they make the changes and do they want to? For example, do they have the knowledge/training they need to make this change? Is it something they want to do? Also, check their social connections. Are friends, coworkers, and others providing positive support by helping, not hindering? Are they giving positive reinforcement by encouraging, not discouraging?

Finally, the systems, processes, culture, organization, and other nonhuman aspects involved in the coaching effort need to support the desired change. For instance, a coach may be working with someone to help them become a better team member—collaborative, supportive, etc.—while the organization continues to reward individual performers.

When coaching is not progressing as desired, work through these questions to get the process back on track.

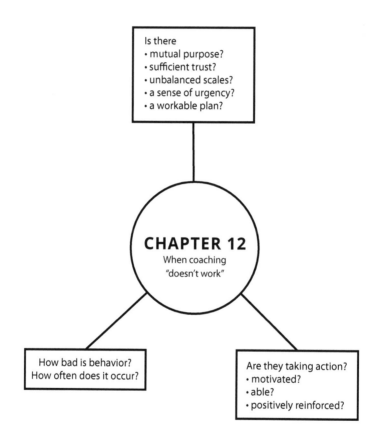

Is there
• mutual purpose?
• sufficient trust?
• unbalanced scales?
• a sense of urgency?
• a workable plan?

CHAPTER 12
When coaching
"doesn't work"

How bad is behavior?
How often does it occur?

Are they taking action?
• motivated?
• able?
• positively reinforced?

13

BUILDING A
COACHING CULTURE

"Instead of waiting for a leader you can believe in,
try this: become a leader you can believe in."

—Stan Slap, organizational consultant and author

We've been focused on providing the know-how for coaches to become competent. In and of itself, becoming a competent coach is worth the effort. Once learned, coaching skills can help anyone be more effective and add value to any of life's roles. Bringing coaching into an organization's culture, so that it is used widely and on a regular basis, will multiply the effectiveness of one coach and positively affect the organization's culture. To this end, we offer a few suggestions for expanding coaching beyond one individual.

CONVERT COACHEES INTO COACHES

RealTime Coaching is a nonmanipulative approach to working with others. That is, the process works whether the person being coached understands the theory and four questions or not.

In a culture with few coaches, where WDIP is not yet widely known, there may be opportunities (often when a person comes to a coach seeking help) for the coach to briefly explain coaching and the four questions. Then the coach can encourage the person to respond to the questions, suggesting that the process may help them gain new insights into their problem. In this case, the coach's role is to listen to the person's answers to make sure they are not fooling themselves or are caught in a blind spot. The coach once again becomes an accountability partner, and the person who is self-coaching becomes even more responsible for the process.

This process has several advantages. It helps the person become more self-aware and self-reliant. It helps the coach's relationship with that person become more trusting. And it leads to more people understanding the WDIP questions and coaching becoming an accepted part of the culture.

USE THE WDIP QUESTIONS FOR PROBLEM-SOLVING

To promote a coaching mindset in an organization, use the four coaching questions as the basis for problem solving. In addition to using WDIP with an individual, WDIP can be used with teams.

For example, when considering a problem, ask *"What do we all want? What would an acceptable solution for all parties look like?"* This is the organizational approach to creating a mutual purpose.

Make sure all sides of the issue are represented when an acceptable solution is discussed. The solution should be stated in terms of "what we want," not "what we don't want." Don't rush this step. Be inclusive. This is the "purpose" step, not the "strategy" step, so do not get hung up on "how" the solution will be created yet. That comes later.

When the group has identified an acceptable solution, ask, *"What are we doing to make that happen?"* This is the "how" step.

Usually there is a gap or difference between what the group wants and what they are doing to get what they want. Otherwise, they would already have the desired solution. The organizational scale is unbalanced. The team uncovers this by asking, *"Is what we are doing getting us closer to our desired solution?"* And, *"Are we moving fast enough?"*

Depending on the answer to those self-evaluation questions, the obvious next question to ask is, *"What do we need to do next? What is our plan now?" "Do we need to make any mid-course corrections?"* And so the process continues. Next, we confirm that what we wanted is still what we want, then we put our next steps into action. As the problem-solving work continues, the team can evaluate its progress.

Using WDIP as a problem-solving process for teams or departments is an effective way to encourage the spread of the four questions and RealTime Coaching into an organization's culture.

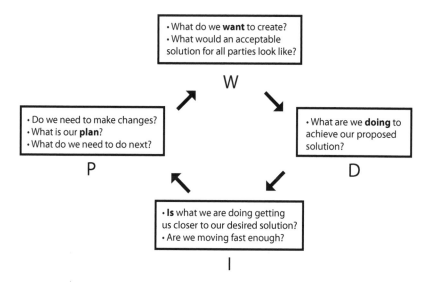

ENCOURAGE PEER-TO-PEER COACHING

When the WDIP questions are used for problem solving, or are otherwise widely known and adopted in a culture, an obvious next step is to encourage their use for peer-to-peer coaching. That is, anyone can assume the role of a coach as a way to provide legitimate help to a peer or co-worker. Often people ask for help and advice on any number of subjects. Sometimes some other person or peer has knowledge or experience and can give valuable advice.

At other times, often when the conversation starts with a comment like, *"How can anybody work with Frank?"* a conversation can quickly turn into a gripe session. *"I know. He's the worst. Let's go get coffee and talk about him."* Both giving advice (Do For) and gripe sessions can have their own negative unintended consequences. Using the WDIP questions can be an effective alternative when someone asks for advice or help.

If becoming a peer accountability partner becomes typical behavior in a culture, it will serve as a positive deterrent to the negative habit of griping and will give people who hesitate to give advice an effective way to support their peers and coworkers.

Anyone can promote the use of WDIP by simply putting the four questions on a sheet of paper and posting them on their wall.

SHARE PERSONAL MOTIVATORS AND BEHAVIORAL STYLES

While basic coaching does not have to involve personal assessments, we believe that both the personal motivators and behavioral styles assessments are valuable for providing insights on three levels: (1) helping people gain a better understanding of themselves; (2) demonstrating that not everyone is motivated by the same things nor do they choose to do things the same way; and (3) showing that it is possible to modify one's behavior to better communicate with and influence (coach) others.

These are valuable insights on their own. When shared with others, they often improve trust and productivity within a team or organization. These assessments are easy to share in a group because they are not a "test." There are no grades. One set of motivators or DISC scores is just as valid as another. In fact, a team with a variety of motivators and behavioral styles is often more effective than one with all one style.

One approach to using assessments with a group is to schedule a team meeting. Most groups use a facilitator who will lead the group through the team members' motivators and behaviors reports. This provides a great opportunity to share information in a supportive manner. Another approach for smaller organizations is to create summary sheets of employees' motivators and behaviors information and make them available to all members of the organization. This approach encourages people to use the assessments routinely, as a part of the culture, instead of seeing them as something that is only looked at during a special event.

WELCOME ABOARD

If a coaching culture exists in an organization, coaching skills should be a part of every manager's toolkit. When a new employee arrives, we recommend setting up a three-way meeting between the new hire, the manager, and a facilitator who can explain the motivators and DISC reports. The manager brings the employee's report and the new hire receives the report. The facilitator then walks the new hire through the reports. This can be done in 60-90 minutes and is a very high-value activity.

At the end of that meeting, both the employee and the manager have a good understanding of how the other person prefers to be communicated with, influenced, and managed. The manager also has a clear picture of the employee's invisible motivators ("wants"), as well as how they prefer to take action ("doing"). This information makes coaching conversations more effective.

Most new employees are appreciative of this meeting and the information they receive. We hear comments like, "Do you do this for all employees?" And, "I would have to have worked here for a year to figure out this information about how to deal with my manager. This way I learned it in an hour."

COACH, DON'T EVALUATE

Organizations are riddled with both personal and systemic evaluation. Assuming, concluding, and judging are second nature to most humans. This carries over into the systems and processes designed by evaluators. Vestiges of an earlier era in organizations (such as annual appraisals, numerical rating and ranking, top-down goals, and 360 reviews) are still common in many organizations. They are all based on someone evaluating someone else.

Coaching is different. Coaching is based on self-evaluation. When coaching is a part of the culture, many of these evaluative policies can be reduced or canceled all together. For instance, there is no need for an annual review, particularly those tied to pay ranges, if it is replaced by supervisors and managers who can and will coach on a regular basis.

Coaching is not necessarily easier than depending on an annual appraisal ritual where a person finds out what management thinks or what number they are. Coaching replaces a systemic process with intrinsic conversations between people. We believe that, particularly in a world where decisions are made quickly and close to where the work is being done, the organizations that have the most brains solving their problems usually win. This collaborative, problem-solving approach is a characteristic of a Do With culture that perfectly emulates the WDIP model. People prefer to be coached than judged. And it turns out that a collaborative approach to dealing with people is better for the financial bottom line as well.

To promote collaboration, coach—don't judge.

BE THE CHANGE YOU SEEK

Now it is up to you. If your intention is to create and sustain a culture of coaching in your organization, then just do it. Take Gandhi's advice, *"Be the change you seek."* If you need help, go back and review this book. Find others who are interested in furthering their coaching skills and talk together. Start small. Coach where you can. Encourage those you coach to be coaches themselves. Support coaching as a key management skill in your organization. Just keep coaching!

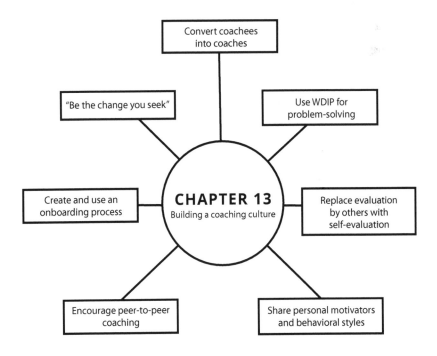

RESOURCES

A person with the right intention and knowledge of the four coaching questions can coach. Combining that skill with assessments to gain additional knowledge about both themselves and the people they coach will make the coach more effective, more quickly.

BASIC NEEDS AND DRIVING VALUES

Our coaching model tells us a person's wants stem from a few basic human needs. Researchers have developed a number of theoretical models of basic human needs. Glasser's four psychological needs and Spranger's six value attitudes are two examples.

Our assessment partners at TTI have developed an easy-to-use online instrument based on Spranger's work. This instrument uses Spranger's six value attitudes as a basis for identifying what a person is attracted to or motivated by and what is not motivating to a person. This assessment makes visible the invisible values that motivate a person's behaviors.

It is not our intention to fully explore the subject of basic human needs here. We offer in-depth training as a part of our coaching workshops. What follows is a short explanation to provide a foundation for understanding how a person's personal motivation influences wants that affect behaviors. Making this connection is foundational for any coach.

Earlier in the book, we mentioned the six value attitudes as identified by Spranger: Theoretical, Utilitarian, Aesthetic, Social, Individualistic, and Traditional. We use six keywords, or motivators, to more clearly define those values: Knowledge, Utility, Surroundings, Others, Power, and Methodologies. A person may be driven by any combination of the six motivators. They may be passionately motivated, moderately motivated, or negatively motivated. The distribution of people around any of the six motivators is basically a bell-shaped curve. The top 15-20 percent are passionate, the bottom 15-20 percent are indifferent and the 60-70 percent in the mainstream are situational toward these particular motivators. Their motivation comes from one or more of the other five values.

Let's use the Theoretical motivator (keyword: Knowledge) as an example. Someone who is highly energized by this motivator is passionate about opportunities to learn and search for the truth. We say they have an Intellectual driving force. On the other end of the Knowledge scale are people who are indifferent to learning for learning's sake. We say they have an Instinctual driving force. They prefer to use intuition, "go with their gut," and seek specific knowledge only when necessary. The Knowledge motivator thus creates two driving forces: Intellectual and Instinctive. Intellectual is the term for those who are passionate about the search for truth. Instinctual is the term for those who are indifferent to or resistant to the search for truth for its own sake. Following is a summary of the six motivators listed with their keywords along with their accompanying twelve driving forces.

THEORETICAL (KNOWLEDGE)—MOTIVATED BY OPPORTUNITIES TO LEARN, DISCOVER TRUTH, AND OBTAIN KNOWLEDGE FOR ITS OWN SAKE

Passionate Theoretical driving force: *Intellectual*

- Traits: Objective, rational, problem solver, lifelong learner, seeks knowledge for knowledge's sake

- Stressors: Lack of learning opportunities, emotional or subjective experiences

- Occupations: Researcher, engineer, medical diagnostician

- Coaching tip: Focus on facts, data, discovery of truth

Indifferent Theoretical driving force: *Instinctual*

- Traits: Uses past experience, intuition, and goes with "gut instinct"

- Stressors: Over-intellectualizing, too much focus on theory, models, proofs
- Occupations: Head coaches, jobs requiring quick decisions
- Coaching tip: Keep facts and data relevant to the situation. Don't refer to theories or models

UTILITARIAN (UTILITY)—MOTIVATED BY PRACTICAL RESULTS, BY A RETURN ON THE INVESTMENT OF TIME, TALENT, AND RESOURCES

Passionate Utilitarian driving force: *Resourceful*

- Traits: Practical, efficient, useful, makes things better
- Stressors: Wasted resources, achievement without reward, wasted time
- Occupations: Salesperson, entrepreneur, CFO, accountant
- Coaching tip: Focus on return on investment, prove "value." Show how an investment of their time and energy will benefit them

Indifferent Utilitarian driving force: *Selfless*

- Traits: Completes tasks for the greater good; doesn't expect a personal return on investment
- Stressors: Too much focus on efficiency, business talk, no focus on others or the planet

- Occupations: Collaborative team member, works for nonprofit
- Coaching tip: Focus on how a change of their behavior can benefit the greater good

AESTHETIC (SURROUNDINGS)—MOTIVATED BY FORM, BALANCE, HARMONY, AND BEAUTY IN THEIR SURROUNDINGS

Passionate Aesthetic driving force: *Harmonious*
- Traits: Appreciates surroundings, subjective, "sees" the whole picture
- Stressors: Objective truth, inability to grow personally, chaotic environments
- Occupations: Artist, gardener, decorator, strategic planner, systems programmer, park ranger
- Coaching tip: Focus on subjective feelings, focus visually on the future; say, "picture this"

Indifferent Aesthetic driving force: *Objective*
- Traits: Driven by the functionality of their surroundings
- Stressors: Too much "fluff," no focus on efficiency, work-life balance
- Occupations: Firefighter, emergency room nurse, crisis manager
- Coaching tip: Compartmentalize the chaos; focus objectively on the main thing

SOCIAL (OTHERS)—MOTIVATED BY HELPING OTHERS

Passionate Social driving force: *Altruism*
- Traits: Selfless, compassionate, caring, serving and benefiting others, generous
- Stressors: Emphasis on bottom line, decisions insensitive to people, individualism
- Occupations: Nonprofits, nurses, elementary school teachers
- Coaching tip: Focus on how their behavior can help others, reduce pain and conflict

Indifferent Social driving force: *Intentional*
- Traits: Assists others for a specific purpose
- Stressors: Too much focus on others, giving to others without getting something
- Occupations: For-profit worker, entrepreneur, repair person, technician, Shark Tank panelist
- Coaching tips: Focus on changing behavior to achieve the desired purpose

INDIVIDUALISTIC (POWER)—MOTIVATED BY POWER, BEING IN CHARGE, FORMING ALLIANCES, AND "CLIMBING THE CORPORATE LADDER"

Passionate Individualistic driving force: *Commanding*
- Traits: Wield power with a purpose, advance personal position, status and recognition; desires personal freedom

- Stressors: Loss of power or position, inability to advance, lack of personal opportunities
- Occupations when combined with other high motivators:
  - Commanding and Resourceful: business owner
  - Commanding and Altruistic: mayor
  - Commanding and Intellectual: dean of a college
- Coaching tip: Focus on how a change of behavior can increase personal power and advance the person, team, or organization

Indifferent Individualistic driving force: *Collaborative*

- Traits: Driven by being in a supporting role, contributing with little need for individual recognition
- Stressors: Leadership situations, presenting, speaking
- Occupations: Customer service, team member, assistant coach
- Coaching tip: Focus on how a change of behavior will help the person better support others

TRADITIONAL (METHODOLOGIES)—MOTIVATED BY TRADITIONAL APPROACHES, DEFINED SYSTEMS FOR LIVING AND METHODOLOGIES.

Passionate Traditional driving force: *Structured*

- Traits: Driven by unity, order, traditions, principles, and methodologies; may have a personal structured system for living

- Stressors: Opposition to personal belief system, change for the sake of change
- Occupations: Minister, police officer, army general, social activist
- Coaching tip: Take time to understand their belief systems and work with them within their system

Indifferent Traditional driving force: *Receptive*
- Traits: Driven by new ideas, methods, and opportunities that fall outside defined systems
- Stressors: "This is how we have always done it," highly structured environments, no wiggle room
- Occupations: Strategist, advertising executive, fashion designer
- Coaching tip: Encourage them to use their creativity to find new ways to solve their problem

These twelve driving forces help us understand the personal motivators driving what people want. Of course, people's motivations are a complex combination of many factors, and we are not attempting to make things simpler than they are. We are saying a valid assessment can help identify the underlying reasons people do what they do. Coaches can use this information to help people better understand what they want and, in turn, what to do to get it.

USING ASSESSMENTS TO UNDERSTAND AND COACH DIFFERENT BEHAVIORAL STYLES

Researchers have developed various models to categorize and explain behaviors. The Myers-Briggs assessment is a well-known model, based on the work of C.G. Jung, the Swiss psychotherapist. It was developed in the early 1960s. We use a different model based on the original research of William Moulton Marston. The common term for this model today is DISC. It uses four factors that, when combined, provide an accurate description of a person's behavioral style. DISC is a mnemonic for Dominance, Influence, Steadiness and Compliance. A number of vendors provide instruments, either paper or online, to measure someone's DISC variables. Our partner and vendor, TTI, offers what we believe to be an excellent, valid, easy-to-use DISC assessment. This is the instrument we use to support the Doing part of the coaching model.

Our intention in this section is to give a short description of the DISC system. We offer in-depth training on the DISC model as a part of our coaching workshops. A person with the right intention can coach if they know the four coaching questions. Understanding the personal motivators and behavioral styles information and assessments can move coaches to a higher level of competence. Coaching basics can be learned in a day or two, while mastering the art of coaching can be practiced and improved for a lifetime.

Suffice it to say a competent coach is good at recognizing different behavioral styles. Following is a short list of characteristics that describe each of the four DISC styles. Each of the four styles refers to a different aspect of behavior. For instance, Dominance describes how someone handles problems and challenges. Compliance describes how people handle rules and procedures set by others. A person's behavior is a combination of all four variables, and the amount of each variable in their behavior may change as the person takes on various roles throughout the day.

Since behaviors are visible, you can probably think of people you know who fall into each of these categories.

DOMINANCE—HOW A PERSON RESPONDS TO PROBLEMS AND CHALLENGES

People who rank high on the dominance scale are extroverted, results-oriented, decisive, quick to act, forceful, and goal-oriented. They love change and challenges. They are risk takers. High dominance is characterized by high expectations of others and being impatient with others. Individuals who demonstrate this behavioral style love competition and challenges and hate routine. They fear being taken advantage of and will therefore choose to "fight" if they sense someone is trying to take advantage of them.

When coaching people with a high dominance style, coaches need to focus on helping them achieve their goals rather than judging or criticizing. (The dominant person will "fight" the judge or critic.) Get right to the subject of the coaching conversation without a lot of chitchat. Watch for impatience as a sign that the coaching is not moving fast enough. Be firm yet not confrontational. Our mantra when working with the high dominance style is, *"Be brief. Be bright. Be gone."*

INFLUENCE—HOW A PERSON ATTEMPTS TO INFLUENCE OTHER PEOPLE

People with a high influence score are extroverted, enthusiastic, confident, and people-oriented. They love to interact with others and prefer to verbally "sell" their ideas. People with low influence scores prefer to influence others with facts and data—to "tell" their ideas. People with high influence scores enjoy social recognition and enthusiastic people interactions. They dislike skepticism and negativity. The high influence style fears social rejection and will choose "flight" when a controversy arises.

When coaching people with the high influence style, allow some time for social conversation while making sure those being coached don't take all the time talking. A person with the high influence style usually enjoys the coaching conversation but tends to be disorganized and may not remember what they agreed to do. We recommend sharing with them a simple written plan and a summary of the coaching session.

STEADINESS—HOW A PERSON RESPONDS TO THE PACE OF CHANGE IN THEIR ENVIRONMENT

People with a high steadiness score are patient, relaxed, steady, modest, and good listeners. They are introverted with a focus on people. They do not like change or risk and have a fear of loss of stability. The high steadiness style is nonemotional. They could be having a great day or a horrible day and others may not be able to tell. People with high steadiness

165

scores strive for closure, well-defined territories, and a chance to serve others. They do not like surprises, insecurity, or lack of closure. They see conflict as a probable loss of stability and so they tend to accommodate or put up with adverse situations rather than confronting and dealing directly with them.

When coaching people with a high steadiness style, coaches should not move too fast or attempt to force a quick response. Be relaxed, calm, and methodical. Allow them time to think. Show interest in them as people. Remember, they do not like change, particularly if there is not a "good reason."

COMPLIANCE—HOW A PERSON RESPONDS TO RULES AND PROCEDURES SET BY OTHERS

People with a high compliance score are neat, conservative, precise, and quality-oriented. They are introverted, task focused, and are direct communicators. High compliance people are driven by rules and procedures. They want to know the rules and don't like it when rules change. This type fears criticism of their work and may tend toward perfectionism. Obviously, they prefer low-risk situations and are concerned about what effect a change may have on them and their work. They like standards, rules, and quality information. They do not like personal criticism, decisions without data, or irrational, emotional feelings. Their approach to conflict is to avoid it.

Coaches working with people who have high compliance scores should be well organized and prepare their case in advance. Coaches need to have their facts and data in order.

Don't try to force a quick decision from someone with a high compliance style. They are already critical of themselves, so coaches should be careful when making any statement that could be construed as criticism of them or their work.

With just a little bit of study, most people are able to identify their own behavioral style as well as that of others. Coaches use this knowledge to improve their communication and influence with others.

ACKNOWLEDGMENTS

This book would not have been published without excellent help from a few wonderful people.

Thanks first and foremost to the infinitely patient and wise Roi-Ann Bettez who turned our fragmented thoughts and ideas into a coherent manuscript that still sounds like us.

The "fine sanding" (line editing) was done with amazing attention to detail by Sallie Showalter and Michelle Johnson. Randy thought he was detail-oriented until he met these people.

We also want to acknowledge all the people who took their time to read our early manuscripts and provided valuable suggestions.

Thanks to Alyssa Patmos for creating the brand identity of RealTime Coaching.

Thanks to Maryanna Young and her team at Aloha Publishing for their help in advancing this manuscript into book form.

Randy has worked with Aloha on two previous books, *Bumper Sticker Leadership: One-Liner Wisdom on Life and Business* and as co-author with Ron Price, *The Complete Leader: Everything You Need to Become a High-Performing Leader*. Both times they fulfilled all expectations and we are delighted they were able to help us again on this project.

ABOUT THE AUTHORS

Randy Lisk enjoyed a twenty-year career with IBM, where he held numerous senior management and leadership roles in engineering and planning. He founded Lisk Associates, a business consulting firm, in 1991. Randy is known as an extremely effective group facilitator, trusted adviser, executive coach, and consultant to businesses. This is the fourth book Randy has authored.

Randy holds a BS degree in electrical engineering from the University of Cincinnati and an MS degree in electrical engineering from the University of Kentucky.

Ryan Lisk is the second-generation owner of Lisk Associates. He has taught RealTime Coaching to hundreds of emerging leaders. Ryan is a certified executive coach for Lee Hecht Harrison and a member of the International Coach Federation. Lisk Associates' clients range from family-owned businesses to Fortune 1000 organizations. His focus is bringing value to clients primarily in the areas of selection and development.

Ryan is certified by Target Training International, Inc. as a professional behavioral, motivators, and TriMetrix analyst. He graduated from the University of Kentucky with a BS in business administration. This is the first book Ryan has authored.

He resides in Sarasota, Florida, with his wife, Angie, and two children, Keensley and Griffin.

Made in the USA
Columbia, SC
13 October 2021